THRESHOLDS TO
GREATER GLORY

Becoming a Vessel of Honor

DR. FRANCES HOUSTON CUFFIE

Parchment Global Publishing

1-888-266-0922
www.parchmentglobalpublishing.com
info@parchmentglobalpublishing.com

Printed in the United States of America

ISBN 978-1-959483-44-1 (sc)
ISBN 978-1-959483-45-8 (e)

Library of Congress Control Number: 2023918827

History
2023.01.09

This book is dedicated
To my United Church Fellowship
International Family

CONTENTS

ACKNOWLEDGEMENTS

I acknowledge all the people who are praying and have prayed and influenced my life.

First, and foremost, to Jesus, the Christ, who is my Lord and Savior, who called, prepared, preserved and poured His Spirit into me.

My beloved grandmother, Ella Clara Houston, who celebrated her 110th birthday, December 25, 2017, who died a month later.

To my deceased husband of forty years, Melvin M. Cuffie, the love of my life.

My pastor, Apostle Dr. Willie B. Williams, who encourages me through the Word and decrees and declares the power of God over and in my life and who teaches me about being in unmitigated rest with the Lord.

My friend, sister and mentor, Pastor Stephanie Callwood, the teacher God sent when I was ready to move forward.

My daughter, Karen Cuffie, who gives me fresh insight each time we speak.

Pastor TaRee Middleton who showed herself faithful to the ministry during our times of need and who has always been there with me in every transition.

My friend and sister-in Christ, Elder Andrea Chapman, who was always "there" for me during my husband's illness and who helped me understand the importance of release.

My prayer partner, travel buddy and best friend, Pastor Adriane Chubb, who keeps me grounded.

My church family, Temple United Church, whom it is a pleasure to lead and is always faithful cheering me on as I follow Christ.

Missionary-elect Henrietta Lee, who was always there to help feed and clothe the less fortunate and who took over that ministry so I could do what God wanted me to do.

Ms. Carole McCreary-Maddox, my law school buddy, who became a friend for life. She encouraged me to continue my studies even when I felt like giving up.

And to all those who provided the soil necessary for me to grow that the insights in this book would touch the life of someone else.

PREFACE

I was asked, "Why are you writing this book. What do you have to offer that people would be interested in knowing"? I have written training materials for the Church for many years. I have never written for the general public. Yet, I knew that the Lord had given me something to say, something that I believe would help someone else get free. I had been successful, through the Word of God, to become free from bondage, free from selfishness, free from depression and free from the penalty of sin. Yes, I have something to say.

The Lord has brought me through many troubling situations. Through many challenges. And, as the old saying goes, through thick and some thin. God has answered prayers of many people whom I have had the pleasure of meeting.

I want to share with you the ability of a true and living God. A true and living Father of all. A loving God that cares for all of us no matter what color, creed, gender or socio-economic group, which we may be included. God loves us. The particular point that I want to make today is, are we seeking to become a vessel of honor before our God or, are we only interested in what He can give us, to satisfy our flesh.

First, I wrote this book to assist others who may have found themselves in similar situations to know that there is hope in the Word of God; there is hope in Christ.

Second, I wrote this book to show that if we seek Him (Christ) first, if we make Him the priority in our lives, He will impart His Holy Spirit within us to give us the power over our enemy, the deceiver.

Third, I wrote this book to show that we can become vessels of honor before Christ. That Jesus paid the ultimate price to free us from the penalty of sin. That the gift of God is eternal life.

INTRODUCTION

"You may not understand today or tomorrow, but eventually God will reveal why you went through everything you did."
- Curiano.com

As you read this quote, did you go back and read it more than once and ponder its meaning? Did you think, well how does this apply to reaching thresholds to greater glory? Did you even think about what this quote might be saying to you, today?

When I saw this quote, I immediately thought of the experiences and events that I endured putting this book together. Getting to this point. For surely, life was not easy. And, I am certain that if you are reading this, life has not been easy for you either.

What I offer you in these few pages is hope. Hope through Christ. Hope that you can complete the journey that has been set before you. That in spite of or maybe, because of, what is happening and what has happened, during your formative years and even now, you can go on. You can be successful. You can come out of this. You must believe that God is a rewarder to them who diligently seek Him. That He is your comfort in times of struggle. That He is a man of His word. He will never leave you, nor forsake you.

You are encouraged to step out in faith. Pick up the paddle of hope and row to the other side of the sea. Take Jesus at his word and cast your net on the other side of the ship so that you may catch blessings, more than you can handle. Be encouraged as you go through life's ups and downs. Be encouraged as you move from one degree of grace into another. Be encouraged when friends doubt what the Spirit of God has been saying to you. Be encouraged to know that you are not alone in this journey.

Realize that no matter what has happened in your past, God has a future of good things for you. Stretch out on faith. So give God praise in spite of the pain, in spite of the disappointment. Thank Him during the struggles. Trust Him when you are tempted to lose hope and love Him when He seems distant and far away. Give God the glory He is due. Do not despise the day of small things. God is still in the delivering business. He is still in the miracle working business. He is still in the loving business.

All of us have failed at some time in our lives. Sometimes we just mess up. Face it but do not stay down. Ask for forgiveness. Learn from the mistakes. Ask God, what am I to learn from this even? By applying the Biblical principles that have been set out in this book, you will be able to overcome the hindrances in your life.

Remember, mistakes happen. Failures happen. But mistakes and failures are what breeds success. Abraham Lincoln endured a steady stream of failure and defeat before becoming the 16th President of the United States. He lost eight elections, twice failed in business and suffered a nervous breakdown but he did not quit. Moses knew going back into Egypt he could be killed since he fled Egypt as a murderer. Why should King Pharaoh release the children of Israel on his say so? He had already been told by God that King Pharaoh would not release the Israelites that easily. Yet, he persevered. Persevere with God. He will reveal to you the whys and the wherefores in due season. But do not faint during the journey. See the face of God as you continue to climb the mountain, as you continue to go through the storm. See His face. Lean on His promises to you.

He is a Deliverer and a Comforter. As you read this, prepare to cross the thresholds to greater glory in Christ.

CHAPTER 1

IN THE BEGINNING

"Nor is new wine put into old wineskins [that have lost their elasticity]; otherwise the wineskins burst, and the (fermenting) wine spills and the wineskins are ruined. But new wine is put into fresh wineskins, so both are preserved."

- St. Matthew. 9:17 Amplified Bible

I knew I was different at an early age. I could see what others could not. I knew things before they occurred. What was wrong with me. My mother was afraid of me. My grandmother chalked up my "stories" as a vivid imagination. I had no friends in grade school or junior high school. I had only two friends during my entire high school years. I thought, Lord, help me. What is wrong with me. Why can't I be like other people my age. Why am I different? Why???

Little did I know that the Lord was working with me and had been working with me since birth. I had not been made aware of the Word of the Lord that was presented by the Prophet Jeremiah in Chapter 29 verse 11 *"For I know the thoughts that I think toward you, saith the Lord, thoughts of peace and not of evil, to give you an expected end."* **KJV** I am the eldest of twelve; one set of twins with me being one of them. My sister and I were born early. We were premature, diagnosed with pneumonia and not being given much hope for survival. My sister did not make it. Yet, I was convinced she was still a part of me. Maybe that is why everyone thought, including me, that I was "different".

We lived with my grandmother. My mother, brothers, sisters, my aunts and cousins, all in one house (let us not forget the other 'family' members that my grandmother would take in from time to time). They were not religious and definitely not Believers as we understand Believers today. My grandmother was a "die-hard Baptist". Let me say, here, that I have nothing against the Baptist beliefs. My Mom did not become a believer in the power of God until years later-try 30 years later. I briefly attended a Catholic church. I believed in the church. Always did. But I had a rude awakening when me and my cousin, who had studied so hard to complete the required readings for Catechism, were turned away from taking our first communion for reasons that did not make sense. The fees were paid that were required. The readings were completed. All assignments were turned in. Suffice it to say, that Catholicism was not for me.

In my heart, even as a child, I knew this was not right. My heart was broken. I had read Psalm 23, where David said, ***"The Lord is my shepherd."*** This attitude from spiritual leaders was not what we were supposed to expect or accept. Something was clearly wrong. I remember crying all the way home. My mom did not have any answers to my questions. I felt alone and unwanted. While my cousin met the same fate, it did not seem to affect her in the same way.

Years later I was sitting in a living room church listening to the pastor give a message to a small, newly formed, congregation. He was really preaching hard. Sweating and moving from one side of the room to the other. The Spirit of the Lord was on him so heavily. The congregation was captured. I was captured.

He said, we are to "reach for the greater glory of God. We are to strive to be a vessel of honor". I remembered the words of that pastor who had preached so strongly. Even now, when it seems like I am at a loss, when it seems like I am alone. When my mind would tell me, " I am not good enough". Intellectually, I knew differently. But emotionally, I was lacking. My faith was not yet strong enough to comprehend what was happening. I wanted to accept the Lord as my strength. I wanted to accept Christ as my Savior. I needed guidance. I could not do it alone.

I kept thinking, how could I be a vessel of honor if I am not allowed to take Communion because of something I had no control over. I felt this pulling. This urging to accept what this pastor was saying. I felt the call of the Lord, God. I felt the love that was being presented on Jesus' behalf.

The issue before me now is, how to get there.

> To say that God is sovereign is to declare that whatever takes place in time is but the outworking of that which He decreed in eternity."
>
> **– A.W. Pink**

How was this to be? What hope did I have of finding Him? Learning and experiencing His truth in my life. How could I become a vessel of honor? Could I ever be 'worthy'? How was I to find this threshold yet alone learn how to cross it?

I pleaded with God, crying and seeking through scripture at night. Talking with ministers and saints whom I met; reading book, after book, after book. Show me the way. Show me what I need. How can I serve you, Lord? I want to be of use to you. I want to win souls for you.

My family moved from the projects in Southwest, in the District of Columbia, to Northeast D.C. It was then, at the age of 12 that I was introduced to God as Lord; Jesus Christ, His Son as my Savior; and the Holy Spirit, the Comforter. It was then that I began my journey of truth to learn as much as I could about this Savior and His love. He is the Messiah, the Promised One that is espoused in the Bible. scripture. It was then that I understood that God is real and not a "figment" of my imagination. The Lord had been working with me and through me since birth. *"**For I know the thoughts that I think toward you, says the Lord, thoughts of peace and not of evil, to give you a future and a hope.**" Jeremiah. 29:11.* But with no one to teach me, I felt lost.

Prior to getting involved in the Pentecostal church I never understood the scriptures. The Catholic church was still holding services in Latin. No wonder I could not understand. But I was not alone. The Baptist church ministers, at that time and in my experience, were telling us to live holy but doing exactly what they were telling the congregation not to do. Again, I was confused. Very confused. I have since discovered that that same attitude is not just in the Baptist church but other church denominations, as well.

Truly, this journey to understand the Truth of the Lord was not going to be easy. But, the Word of the Lord, did not say it would be. Jesus said, we will have trials, but if we are believers in Him and have faith, we will not go through them alone. He will be with us.

I had no real knowledge of the move of God. I had no teacher to explain how God moves in and through people When my grandmother was short on money (which was every day), she would ask me to give her the number for the day. I would give her "the number". She would play the number and "hit". We ate dinner that day. I had no idea that what I was doing was wrong. Although, I knew it did not feel good to me. Every time I gave her the number, it would make me unhappy.

Somewhere, deep inside I knew God was calling me. I just did not know how to answer Him. I had so many questions.

God is still pouring out His Holy Spirit-the Holy Ghost, today. To whomever is willing to receive Him. Are you ready? Are you just a little bit more curious to understand this threshold? This new level in Christ? The higher heights and deeper depths of the Lord? This was the message that was preached the Sunday that I attended this new church. What did the preacher mean, when he said, "God is pouring out His Holy Spirit-the Holy Ghost"? It is the Holy Ghost that keeps us from falling into temptation. It is the power of the Holy Ghost that enables us to move from one good degree of grace into another.

I had already accepted Christ as my personal Saviour. Did I not receive the Holy Spirit already? What is he saying?? What am I missing? Is this why you sent me here, Lord to open up my mind to receive more. There is more, right?? Obviously, I had no real clue about this theory or interpretation that the minister was offering. The Holy Ghost??? The Holy Spirit??? Are they the same? This concept was not taught in the Catholic church in this way. The words were familiar but the concept was lost to me.

The "Comforter, the Keeper". I had read the scriptures before. But today, today this scripture took on new meaning. I began a search to learn more about this "Comforter, this Keeper". Yes, this Comforter has gender. He is a He. Jesus explained it this way. **"But when the Comforter comes, whom I shall send to you from the Father, the Spirit of truth who proceeds from the Father, *He* will testify of Me"**. St. John 15: 26 KJV

Wow, what a revelation. The Holy Spirit is real. He is our Comforter. He was sent by Jesus to cover us after Jesus' crucifixion. He is the third person of the Trinity.

God is still pouring out His Holy Spirit –the Holy Ghost, today. He is still offering us, The Comforter. Was I ready to really receive Him? Somewhere along the way, I had gotten sidetracked. I realized the need to seek a refresher; to be in His presence and His power; to be strengthen in the Body of Christ.

I remember walking up to the front to accept the minister's offer of Christ in my life. I was twelve but I knew this was right. I felt it in my bones. I had accepted Christ as my personal Savior but there was still something missing. I knew in my spirit that there had to be more. If I am to accept Christ in my life, if I allow Him to take control, then the preacher said, I shall have peace; I shall be able to receive what He (the Lord) determined is my "future".

Yes, I was attending regular Sunday church services. I never missed Sunday School, Bible study or even Friday night services, but there was still something missing.

> "Ask, and it shall be given to you, seek, and you shall find, knock and it shall be opened to you."
> **– St. Matthew 7:7 KJV**

I knew that I was to be a vessel for the Lord. I knew, that more, importantly, I *wanted* to be a vessel for God. I wanted to cross the threshold to receive God's glory. I just did not know how to get there. It became my passion. I made it my destiny in life, to find out.

I did not want to be "dry". I knew that in Christ was life. He said it in His Word. I had visited several churches. Not joined, but visited. I was membered to one church for thirty-four years. I had seen many things and experienced much over the years. But there was still something missing.

My grandmother did not understand what I was trying to tell her. She answered me in the only way she knew how. "Keep asking, the Lord will provide."

As a preteen, I was an advent reader. I lived in a fantasy world. My real world was disappointing. There appeared to be no hope aside from my dreams. *Pippi Longstocking*, by Astrid Lindgren, was my favorite book. I enjoyed Pippi's travels and adventures. I would sit in class and write short stories with Pippi in mind. This activity got me in trouble. My teachers thought I was just day-dreaming. They did not realize I was merely trying to escape the life I was in. I had a gift for writing. At that time, I did not know how much of a gift or even that it was a gift. I dreamed about having a better life; enjoying other cultures; trying new foods. Well, let me be real... sleeping on a mat not wearing hand-me-down cloths or going to bed hungry.

As I continued to grow and pursue my reading, as I stood in the line waiting to sign up for my first library card I realized I was shaking with excitement. I listened to the librarian explain the instructions for use and return of books. I could borrow up to five books at a time. What a rush. I was so excited I overstayed my time at the library. But it was worth the scolding when I returned home. All I could think about was my adventures and the opening of the world that was in front of me. I was unstoppable! I read everything. Fantasy, American history, adventure, prose, poetry, music history, monsters (in particular, vampires), even the dictionary. Wow! I was in "second heaven". I wanted to become a writer. While in high school I wrote the graduating class play, directed and stared in it. It was the happiest day of my life.

Then I discovered Bible history. Adam and Eve. The Garden of Eden. Jesus of Nazareth. In particular, Jewish history. I wanted to know why the Jews celebrated and honored the tabernacle and the Temple, as they did. I wanted to know the significance of the Communion. The mysteries that I learned, the understanding that grew in my spirit after learning the wisdom of these special people made me ravenous for more. The more I took in, the more I applied the understanding of these wise masters, the more I valued the nuggets of precious gold found in this material.

Wow, I never knew the Bible was so interesting. The material I found was beginning to feed the hunger…that empty space. My mind and heart were open to receive whatever revelations God was offering. I felt that it was my duty to seek the threshold to becoming a vessel of honor. I wrote plays for the youth to perform in the church. Even helping the children and youth with making their costumes and scenery from whatever scraps we could find. It was truly uplifting for all.

I started a church newsletter. Writing stories and articles that would be signed by the Pastor. I created puzzles and word challenges for our youth page. God is good. I was excited to share this wonderful knowledge about honoring God.

I was not a preacher or a formal teacher at that time. I just knew that I had a message to deliver and that was the only manner in which I knew how to deliver the gospel of peace. I thought, maybe, I could write children's books to start getting the Word to the children at an early age. I even talked with my husband about my idea, but he was not for that. So, I moved on to seek more of Him and change my own life. I wanted more of God's Word. More of His presence. I vowed, in my heart, to learn more about honoring God with the first fruits of all my increase, with the first fruits of my being.

This journey took me on a road I never knew existed. Realizing that God calls us to a deeper relationship with Him has truly changed how I think about Him and how I react in and outside His presence. It also taught me that I must be cognizant of how I treat my fellow man. The show of love must be real, not painted on; not fake. It is now my passion; my goal to help others find this great connection.

Seeking this connection requires us to become cleaner, stronger vessels that can hold the power, hold the wisdom, hold the revelation that can only be provided by the Lord. This powerful presence must be kept securely in our hearts. His presence is truly a treasure to be sought after. Being in His presence is more precious than gold. David wrote in Psalm 19:9-10, **"The fear of the Lord is clean, enduring forever: the judgments of the Lord are true and righteous altogether. More to be desired are they than gold, yea, than much fine gold: sweeter also than honey and the honeycomb."** *(KJV)*

Many times, when we ask, "Are you ready to receive Christ as your personal Savior", the response is "when I get myself together, I will come to church". Little do we know that "we" can never get "ourselves together". If that were the case, we would not need Christ. He would not have had to die. However, we are encouraged to accept Christ. Accept to be led by His word and receive the Holy Spirit within.

It is important, no, it is imperative that we accept Christ as our personal Savior now. We cannot take the chance to wait until "we get ready". Time waits for no man. Accept Him. Let Him help us get ready. He will clean us up and place us in His cool place. Once we come into His presence He embraces us with the warmth of His Spirit.

The scripture talks about wine, which also represents the blood of Jesus that was shed for us at Calvary. A wine (blood) that gives life. A wine that is Life. (Author's emphasis added) Wine, as it matures, has to be kept in a tightly covered container in a cool, dark environment. Remember, Jesus' first miracle? Where he turned water into wine at the wedding supper? He used vessels that had been ceremonially cleansed waiting to be used. Because Jesus was part God, He did not have to wait years for grapes to grow, mature and become wine. He was the wine and by His word, the water became what He needed it to become.

The Lord leads us, to "pastors after His own heart". These pastors are expected and prepared to lead us to Christ. These pastors are given

God's direction and understanding of His word to help us prepare ourselves to become the vessels He (God) needs when He is ready for our use.

Once we accept Christ as our personal Savior, we must learn about sanctification. It would be a mistake to stop at salvation. Salvation is like getting in the shower. But after getting in the shower, we must use soap to get cleansed. Sanctification is the "getting cleansed"; the separating ourselves for being set apart for use. But let's not get ahead of ourselves.

Learning to live for Christ is so very important. Sometimes it requires us to be placed 'on a shelf', after being properly cleansed, to await our call for service. Yet, the waiting process does not mean doing nothing. It means being preserved for a specific purpose. Sounds a lot like sanctification to me.

There are times when the enemy will use our time of waiting as an opportunity to discourage us. Instead, I encourage you as Paul encouraged the church at Corinth, "**to stay steadfast and unmoveable, always abounding in the work of the Lord**". 1 Corinthians 15:58 KJV

For this cause, the Lord preserves us. Like wine, that has to be protected until its due time, so do we need protection. That is why it is important that we understand why wineskins had to be used, cleaned and preserved. Handled properly in order to be used to hold the precious liquid to be poured into them. A liquid that continues to have life that bubbles over with richness; fullness of joy.

The preacher's message on sanctification began something like this, 'Sanctification is the setting apart for a specific purpose.' God calls us to be set apart for His use. We must remember this. This means denying self; the flesh. Do not panic. This does not mean we should not put aside nest eggs for our future, nor does it mean we should not create whatever we need to leave a legacy for our families. It does mean that we are to think about where our souls will spend eternity. It means that we should lay up treasures in heaven. We will not be able to take the treasures of this world with us when we die.

We are encouraged to put our hope in Christ.

Never stop learning, because life never stops teaching. The Spirit of the Lord is continually teaching and guiding us into truth. We are urged to listen, really listen. We are taught to listen but be prepared to respond. I urge you to listen to hear and receive; not be quick to respond.

Jesus was not quick to respond. In fact, during the entire time He was being beaten and ridiculed, the scripture says, He did not utter a word. He only spoke when it was time to speak. "Father forgive them for they know not what they do." For example. There are six other utterances (sayings) that we teach and preach on during the Resurrection season. It is truly the Spirit of the Lord that gave Him and gives us the attitude and strength to not speak unless it is absolutely necessary. And when we speak, it ought to be to provide hope and a blessing.

CHAPTER 2

THE HUNGER

"And Jesus said to them, "I am the bread of life. He who comes to Me shall never hunger, and he who believes in Me shall never thirst."

– St. John 6:35 KJV

Have you ever been really hungry? I mean rea…lly hungry? Especially when you know what your taste buds are calling for and nothing else will suffice. If you want Kentucky Fried Chicken, McDonald's, Burger King, Olive Garden, whatever, will not cut it. It must be Kentucky Fried Chicken; nothing less.

Well, I had that same strong, desire for a Word from the Lord. Not just a word, but a capital "W" word. My soul was hungry. It needed to be fed and fed with strong meat from the Word of God. A friend invited me to a revival when one of the ministers from her church was the guest preacher. It so happened that the preacher was Evang. Rita Twiggs. I had heard that she was long winded. Can I say that here. But I also heard that she was a powerful preacher and teacher of the Word. You need to know that I did not, nor do I presently like driving. But hunger, true hunger results in unusual reactions. So, I drove the hour and a-half to be in this service.

It was well worth the hour and a-half drive. Trust when I tell you. If you are truly hungry for the Word of God, if you seek Him, you will find Him. When Jesus was teaching the sermon on the mount, Jesus said to the multitude **"Ask, and it shall be given you; seek and ye shall find; knock, and it shall be opened unto you: For everyone that asketh receiveth; and he that seeketh, findeth; and to him that knocketh it shall be opened. "**

St. Matthew 7:7-8 (KJV). The power of the Lord that was emanating from the preacher in that place was astonishing! Developing a closer relationship with God requires spending time; devoted time with Him. Sometimes it is necessary to drive a little bit to feed that hunger. We make sacrifices for a lot of things in our lives, but we are reluctant to make a sacrifice to learn about or be near the power of God. I remember her words, 'there is someone here today that has pressed their way because they are hungry'. I was sure she was speaking directly to me! I looked around. Feeling that all eyes were on me. But no one was looking at me. They were eating up the meal that was being placed in front of them, just as I was.

God had gotten my attention. Yes, there were other people in the church, about 200 people, to be exact. When the Lord has a message for you, no matter how many other people may be around, you will know it's for you.

The scripture she read, struck me deeply. I felt like I had been kicked in the center of my gut. ***"Blessed are those who hunger and thirst for righteousness, For they shall be filled."*** St. Matthew 5:6 KJV. I had read this scripture at least one hundred times, if not more. How had I missed this? And maybe I had not, it was just not my time. But today! This is the hour to hear.

Suddenly, it struck me that I still had a lot to learn about worshiping the Lord. I had so much to learn about how the Lord desires to be worshipped. I needed to learn how to show Him that I love Him. I had not yet fully given everything to the Lord! I thought I had. But reality brought me back to life. Wake up, little girl. Wake up! No, I was not committing any open sins. But failure to have faith is a sin, by itself. So I needed to start over.

Paul, the Apostle, preached about this same attitude to the church. Sometimes we have been "in" the church so long, we forget that the church is us. We think we know everything there is to know about church. Well, let me share this with you… you may know where the bathrooms are; you may know where the basement light switch is; you may even know where the extra tissues and paper towels are kept. But, we do not know church.

Church is more than the building in which we worship. Church is the attitude of gratitude. Giving gratitude to God for being our Lord. Giving God thanks for our Peace. Giving God thanks for Who He is. Glorifying Him because He is our Lord. Glorifying Him because He is our Keeper. Glorifying Him because He is our Elohim.

Can I say this??? Well, too late now. We can have church with the Lord while cooking dinner; washing dishes, scrubbing floors. It is a good thing; no, it is a great thing to experience God in this manner. Let Him visit you while you serve. It works for me. Remember, it is through service that we learn how to serve; it is through service that we learn the love of God. Just because you can get a prayer through at home does not relieve us from the reminder 'not to forget to assemble ourselves together', to encourage each other.

Church is not the physical building. It is the mindset of being grateful for everything that happens in our lives. It is being grateful for the people we meet. The things we share; the things we learn each day. Let us not forget that it is when we give thanks, when we show our gratitude for what we have received and what mischief has passed us by, that we understand what church is about. It is the mindset of giving God thanks for being who He is in our lives. Our Lord of Lords. King of Kings. The shade upon our right hand. He said, he would be around us like the mountains that are around Jerusalem. We are protected by Him. For He dispatches his angels to take charge over us.

Taking it one step further, even when things happen that do not make us feel good, it is the net result of gratitude that brings relief in such trying times. Try it sometimes. Test the water.

The Apostle Paul said, in his epistle (letter) to the church in Rome, ***"And that knowing the time, that now it is high time to awake out of sleep; for now is our salvation nearer to us than when we believed."*** Romans 13:11 KJV

Have you ever thought to yourself, I keep coming to church, Sunday after Sunday; service after service but I still feel like something is missing? Many times, I hear, ' I grew up in the church. My mother took me with her all the time. When I got old enough, I stopped going.' Sometimes we have been "in the way" so long we think we are alright. Only to find out that we have truly been "in the way" of someone, including ourselves, reaching God in the beauty of holiness. Paul said, "It is now time to awake out of sleep".

Some of us have been in, or more appropriately, around the church for years. We know all the songs, we know how to move and when to move; how to bow and when to raise our hands. But do we know God? Do we really know Jesus, as Lord and Savior of our lives?

There will be a moment of awakening. Pray for it! Seek for it! Go after it!! There comes a moment of truth when we realize we are not all that and a bowl of chips. There are higher heights and deeper depths in Christ, Jesus. Where there is a void in our lives, we need to let Him fill it.

I developed a hunger for more of God. I could not sleep. I could not eat. Nothing satisfied me. I cried, Lord there is a void in my life. I am going to Sunday School. I did not miss Bible Study. I attend all the services, and yet, I felt a void. I felt so alone.

What I did not understand was that the Lord was answering my prayer. He was awakening me from my sleep. I had become complacent with my life and my life with Him until that date with destiny; that revival that woke me up to reach for more.

Now that I have your attention, may I share this personal experience with you? I went to a Christian bookstore and while I was walking the aisles, I heard my name being called. I looked around, thinking that I would see someone I knew in the store. No one. I continued searching the shelves. I was looking for a book that I thought would feed my hunger; feed my aloneness. Again, I heard my name. I looked around. No one. Suddenly, I was halted by a book. It appeared to glow. I felt like Moses must have felt when he saw the bush on fire but not burning. This book called my name. It was John Ortberg's book, "If You Want to Walk on Water You've Got to Get Out of the Boat" (Zondervan Publishing House, 2001). What was happening? I looked up to see if anyone else was experiencing the same thing. Maybe there was a television in the ceiling. Looking around, there was nothing. No one was near me. I moved away from that particular section of the store.

Was I running away from what I asked God to do in my life? Was I racing to get out of the store because I thought I was "hearing" things? Did I have a fever? I felt my head. No, fever. I did not know what to do. I headed toward the door of the store to go out. As I continued pass other bookshelves, I heard my name being called, yet again. This time, the shelf in front of me was empty. Was my mind playing tricks on me? I know I have a vivid imagination, but this was really happening.

At that time, I felt a touch. I was not sure if I should turn around or keep walking. I stopped. I thought one of the clerks had touched me. There was no one. It was then that I realized it was the Lord. A warmth came over me. I returned to the aisle holding the missive that was Mr. Ortberg's book.

With trembling hands, gingerly I picked up the book as if it were hot coals. This book, this inanimate object, could not speak, yet it called my name. I read the back cover and the words resonated in my mind as I read, "Deep within you lies the same faith and longing that sent Peter walking across the wind-swept Sea of Galilee toward Jesus." My heart was totally captured. The Lord had my attention. He heard my prayer. He answered my plea.

In those few moments, I finally understood that I wanted to be a vessel of honor. Not just a vessel to be used but a vessel that has been thoroughly cleansed by the mighty Word and power of God. I wanted to be led and fed by the Lord. I wanted to be one of the vessels he uses when he needs something to hold the new wine. I wanted God! And still do.

I sank to the floor, crying and holding Mr. Ortberg's book. This was not a time to have pride. This was not a time to look around to see who was looking. A clerk came over and asked me if I was alright. I said, through tears of joy, yes. Finally, yes. I said to her, "I can be a vessel of honor". I was so thankful this was a Christian bookstore with real believers who worked here. Believers who understood a move of God. The owner of the store came over and we prayed together, right there in the store. She sat on the floor with me as the presence of the Lord overshadowed both of us.

People began to join in and pray and give God praise. Truly the Lord had orchestrated this opportunity. It was not just for me. It was for anyone who was there who had cried out, seeking more of Him. I felt that He used me to allow others to open up as well.

The Lord had awakened me out of my sleep; my slumber. No longer will I believe the lie of the devil that I cannot be what God has said I could be. I no longer believe the lie that the enemy tried to get me to live. God is my King. Jesus is my Savior. Jesus answered my prayer. Truly, if we hunger and thirst after righteousness, we shall be filled.

CHAPTER 3

THE JOURNEY

"For My people have committed two evils: They have forsaken Me, the fountain of living waters, and hewned themselves cisterns, broken cisterns that can hold no water."
– Jeremiah 2:13 KJV

Seeking this connection to be with the Lord; to be all that I could be in Him, made me realize that from birth I had been called. Let me explain.

I had to come to myself, as the prodigal son did. I thank God I was not actually fighting with the pigs for corn cobs but I was still lost. I heard a voice in my head saying, 'wash your face'. What?? It repeated itself. 'wash your face'.

Sometimes it seems like life just does not go our way; no matter what we do. I know you have had the similar thoughts. Sometimes it appears that there is no end in sight. Ah, may I take this moment to share something with you. Something that will give you hope? Something that will lift your spirit?

I heard you thinking, 'what can lift my spirit'? What is she talking about? What can she offer that I have not already tried? I have no control over my life. Actually, you do. God does not force us to accept Him. He offers us life. In fact, Jesus said, "**I came that you might have**

life and that more abundantly." St. John 10:10 So, we do have choices. We do have control over how we react to circumstances and situations.

Stop crying. Get up! Wash your face! Let's get started.

Count your blessings where you are. One, you are still alive. If you think you have nothing to be grateful for, check your pulse. Stop feeling sorry for yourself. Scripture reminds us, "**For all have sinned and come short of the glory of God**." Romans 3:23. Yes, we were all born in sin and shaped in iniquity. Because of Adam and Eve's sin we were all placed in the same pocket. It was the voluntary death and shedding of the blood of Christ and His powerful resurrection that liberated us. It was His sacrifice that gives us an opportunity to have life. Not how 'good' we are; not on our good looks; not on our education but on His (Jesus') sacrifice alone. So wash your face and move forward.

Two, you have been called for such a time as this. I am the eldest of twelve children. One set of twins—but does that 'really' matter. You might say, what does that have to do with your journey and finding God. Just wait. Be patient. My sister and I (twin) were born premature weighing in at a strapping welter-weight of 1-1/2 and 2 pounds, respectively. My mother was a teenager when she gave birth to us. She was still trying to "find" herself so she had no time for children. After being born, my sister and I developed pneumonia and began our stay in the hospital. We were not given much time to live. My grandmother, the matriarch of our family, became our Mom. The hospital called for my mother to take us out of the hospital or pay her last respects. My mother did not come to the hospital to get us nor to "pay her last respects".

My grandmother, who is now deceased, broke all the rules to get us. She and one of her friends (they were affectionately called "The Lone Ranger and Tonto") came to the hospital. However, before she arrived, my sister passed. She signed me out. The "Lone Ranger and Tonto" hailed a cab and road off into the projects. In her own inimitable way, she had the cab driver drive on the grass (a violation of the law in the projects) and back up to the door of the house to keep the rain off me as she proceeded to prepare to "save" my life. Tell me that this is not the hand of God.

This is where life changed for me. Through the direction of the Lord, my grandmother cared for me and learned how to handle this little tiny baby who did not even know she was in this world. This was truly the first miracle of my life. No one expected me to live. But God had His hand on me even then.

At the age of five, my cousin and I entered elementary school. Sometime during that time, my aunt, my cousin's mother, went missing. I remember when we returned from school, we were told that her mother was missing. It seemed like everyone in our house, the neighbors, and friends were searching the neighborhood without success. I can remember going to my mother and trying to get her attention because I "knew" where they should look. She ignored me. I went to the next person, again, I was ignored. "Move little girl". I remember this so distinctly as if it were yesterday. As the evening went on, it grew dark. I felt the strong need to get someone to listen to me. I went to my grandmother, pulling on her apron (something she wore all the time) and I remember saying, "Look behind the trash cans in the alley." She told one of the men who was in the house, to go check the alley; check behind the trash cans. The person said, "we have already looked there". She raised her voice, which is something she rarely did. She said, 'the girl said look behind the trash cans, she is there." They went. My aunt was discovered. She had been stabbed and had lost a lot of blood. The ambulance was called. She lost a lung but she survived. Only by the grace of God could she have lived.

That day became a day of reckoning for me. "I know where she is". How did I know that? I had not been out. It was late at night. I would not have been playing in the alley even if were daylight. How?? How??

My grandmother asked me how I knew. I said, "I do not know." I just knew". From that day forward, I knew that there was truly something different about me. My grandmother started asking me to give her the number for the day so she could play it. I would give her a number. She played it. Each time, she "hit" the number. We ate.

How did I know I had a "gift ". More importantly, in my head, I felt like it was being misused. I kept rationalizing that it was okay. It was not wrong to do what I was asked to do. I was helping my family. We had food. The electricity was on. Do you know what it's like to have to live in the dark. To have to heat water on firewood outside to bring inside to bathe. Seriously, everything had to be done while it was daylight because we had no electricity. School work was done by candlelight and lanterns. Do you know what it's like to have to wash clothes in a tin tub in the backyard? We did not own a washing machine. Even the water used to wash our clothes had to be heated on wood outside in the backyard. What I was doing was right, right? As I got older, I began to doubt that I was doing a good thing. I began to feel badly about my actions. I had nothing to support that feeling other than my heart was heavy. I was a little girl who "knew" things.

I talked with my grandmother about my feelings. I told her I was very uncomfortable about giving her "the number". I had no spiritual or religious reasons to share. I just felt that it was wrong. She did not give me scripture. She did not give me any profound words of wisdom. She just merely said, very quietly, I will not ask you again if you do not feel comfortable about this. She never did. Yes, there were other times we had no electricity and there were times we had only gravy and homemade biscuits to eat. But we were family. We had each other. We were loved. And we knew it! I knew I was born and survived for such a time as this.

Three, you were given the ability to think and analyze. Sometimes the journey to truth, the journey to discovery, takes us through rough waters, over mountains and through the forests. Sometime through desert places. Dry places. Arid places. It is this journey that builds our faith. It is this journey that we discover who we truly are. Do not despise the journey. For it is through the journey we find the discovery.

Even as children we learn right from wrong. Do not underestimate young children's emotional state. Listen to them. Ask the Lord to let you "hear" what they are saying, not what you are trying to interpret.

CHAPTER 4

THE POTTER'S TOUCH

"And the vessel He was making of clay was spoiled in the potter's hand, and he reworked it into another vessel, as it seemed good to the potter to do so."

– Jeremiah 18:4 (ESV)

I knew something was missing. I knew something was wrong. What I did not know was how to fix it. What was "it" any way? No one had yet sat me down to talk about God. I only knew what I heard from going to church with my grandmother. But I had nothing to relate the words to. God had not become real to me, yet. For it seemed to me that everything the preacher said, don't do, my family did. So how could I believe what I was hearing and watching their actions, was that the correct interpretation? It did not make sense. But I knew things. Things that only God could reveal. I just did not know how I knew.

With this gift comes responsibility. First, recognizing that there is a power that is mightier than you that gives the gift. I had heard the story of the Potter and His clay. Now, at the age of fifteen, it was beginning to make sense.

Now, I did not know what the Prophet Jeremiah was really talking about at that time. I have since learned that we have all sinned and come short of the glory of God. I did not know how to fix what was broken.

At the age of twelve we moved to a different part of the city where I met a young minister and his family who were just starting a church. I attended. I liked it. I liked it a lot! I was learning the Word of God.

The church was in his living room. We began to grow and moved to the basement of the house. My grandmother called it, a "holy roller" church. Another nickname for the holiness movement, I learned. It did not matter to me. I was getting answers to my questions. I was getting fed. I was experiencing a feeling of peace and comfort that I had not experienced in the past. The spirit on the inside of me was being fed and it liked what it was receiving.

I still did not know, yet the full meaning of receiving the Holy Ghost or Holy Spirit as the polite and more polished saints call Him now. I only knew that this is what my spirit was searching for.

Seek the Artesian well that is Christ. Remember the Samaritan woman who encountered Jesus at Jacob's well? The Apostle John penned this story so eloquently. She did not realize that the person she was speaking with was also the water He requested. What a word is this! He said to her, "Give me to drink" in verse 7 of the 4th chapter, and yet in verse 10, He tells her, "If you knew the gift of God, and who it is that says to you, Give me to drink; you would ask of him, and he would give you living water. " [author's emphasis added]. Her cistern was broken. Her sins were exposed to her. Yet, here she stood before the Christ (the Savoir) offering her hope. She accepted.

You are encouraged to seek for the living fountain of water that comes from Christ. Jesus said, "**I came that you might have life and that more abundantly**." For it is only through His resurrection that we have life and that more abundantly". St. John 10:10 Just as plants, trees, grass and our living bodies require water for life, our spirit requires the living water that only Christ can give. Let Him repair the break. Let Him heal that broken spirit. Stop resisting.

Delaying. Procrastination. "Getting myself together". These are all distractions for holding off making the decision to accept Christ as our personal Savior. Stop running. Even though the author of the Book of Hebrews is not certainly known, it does not negate the power of the

Word, "While it is said, "Today if ye will hear his voice, harden not your hearts, as in the provocation." Hebrews. 3:15 KJV

There are consequences to unbelief. Try reading, Hebrews, chapter 4, verses 1and 2. So that you do not have to stop, let me lay it out for you.

> "Let us therefore fear, lest, a promise being left us of entering into his rest, any of you should seem to come short of it. For unto us was the gospel preached, as well as to them: but the word preached did not profit them, not being mixed with faith in them that heard it."
>
> **– KJV**

But let's not get ahead of ourselves. I am encouraging you to seek the purpose that God has for you. Recognize that something is missing in your life. Something may even be broken. But it is the Creator that is the only one who can repair His vessel. No one else can.

Yes, He uses others. He uses us. His creations to help get the word out that He saves. That He heals. That He is our deliverer. That He brings peace.

Yes, we are cracked. We are marred. But in the hands of the Potter, we can be restored.

This morning, when I awoke, I asked the Lord to give me an inspirational message. I also ask Him to help me to be an encourager to someone each day. But today was different.

We never know where our blessings will come from. They do not always come from family and friends. God uses whomever is available. A minister friend delivered food to me for two families for Thanksgiving. I had tried to deliver them the next day but no one was home. I had to think of another opportunity to deliver this food while it was fresh. Because I knew that on my off day, I had to write, I decided I would get up early, deliver the baskets and then return to write. My aim was to stay focused and met my deadlines.

Never measure your progress using someone else's ruler.

– averstu.com

While I was out delivering the food baskets the Spirit of the Lord said, ask this person to ride with you. I said, ride where? I was going home to write so that I could stay focused and meet my deadline. But I did ask the young lady and she was ready and waiting when I arrived. We arrived at our designation and took the food in the house. After praying as we were leaving the house of the recipient, the young lady I picked up said, where are we going? I said, I do not know yet. Let's see what God has in store. I feel that He wants to show me something.

I reached for my phone, opened it and saw Arundel Mills. Now, had been to Arundel Mills with someone else driving but never had I driven myself. I had tried to reach Arundel Mills once before, with me driving and the same person riding shot gun. Needless to say, we never made it. We got lost. But because the Lord spoke, today, we never missed a turn. It pays to hear, correctly, from the Lord.

When we reached our destination we pulled into the parking lot where the theatre is located. Neither of us had ever been to this theatre before. The outside looked like an Egyptian Temple. The hieroglyphics were amazing. It felt like being in Egypt, the Country. Of course, my mind being what as active as it is, I felt like Moses going back into Egypt after hearing the Lord say, "Go tell Pharaoh, to free my people." But this was not Egypt. This was a mall. More particularly, it was the entrance to the theatre section of the mall. As soon as we entered the doors to the mall, the smell of popcorn smacked us in the face. I said, we should make sure we get popcorn to eat on the way home. We were not going into the theatre.

We walked the mall. Just looking and talking with people. Seeing what the stores were offering for the holiday season, listening to Christmas carols. Yes, it is still November, before the Thanksgiving Holiday. What was the purpose of our being there. We still had no idea. So we kept walking. We walked more than half the mall. Waiting for the Lord to direct us.

We stopped to eat lunch where we were witnessed saying our grace by a young Hispanic man who sat with us for a few minutes and joined in. After a few minutes, his friend arrived and they moved to another table after offering a blessing over us. The Lord had begun to work. He let us know that He is not a respecter of people. That it is not necessary that you wear a dress, a skirt, or a suit. That you can wear pants, jeans or overalls and still give God thanks.

Each of us becomes a vessel of service in our own way. No one made fun of, or belittle the other because we looked differently, or dressed differently or of a different nationality.

We ate and talked about the move of God in our respective lives. We talked about the weather of the day. We talked about our desires both for our natural lives, our spiritual lives, our emotional lives and our financial lives. We are made up of more than one side or one dimension. We talked about our deliverance through Christ. Overcoming the hand of the accuser in and over our lives.

Our strength comes from Revelation 12: 11 "And they overcame him by the blood of the Lamb, and by the word of their testimony; and they loved not their lives unto the death." It is by the shed blood of Jesus that we are protected.

We still did not know why we were at this mall. Surely, it was not necessary to drive an hour just to get a sandwich. Surely it was not necessary to drive an hour to say grace over our meal there. What did He (God) have in store?

As we were leaving the mall, we headed in the direction of the theatre where we came in. The smell of popcorn, again, assaulting our senses. I proceeded to approach the ticket counter and inquired as to whether or not we could just go in and purchase popcorn. The gentleman say, "Oh, by all means. Just let the young lady know that you want to purchase popcorn".

We followed the roped off area and entered the doors to the theatre. There sitting in a motorized wheelchair was a very pleasant young (older) lady with the prettiest smile, the most beautiful attitude I had ever encountered. We stopped to chat. Her speech was not perfect, she could not straighten herself up, but she was obviously full of love and gratitude. She was working. She was making a difference. She was able to express herself. She was not ashamed of how she looked to anyone else. I saw the Spirit of the Lord all over her. She exuded a confidence in her spirit that I had not seen for some time and never in anyone who was living with what we call challenges.

I believe God wanted me to witness her enthusiasm for life. That it was important to see that no matter what state we find ourselves, we can still give Him glory but showing the Love that God is.

We were told that her name is Jan. Truly she is a vessel of honor. She never had to say, I'm a Christian. She never had to say, I love the Lord. Nor did she say, I am a believer. The presence of a faithful God, a loving God, a peaceful God was all over her.

Never underestimate the value of your vessel. What we may see as marred in our eyes is not marred in God's eyes. Our Creator, our Heavenly Father has a way of using what we consider our imperfections for His glory. Truly Jan is a vessel of honor.

Even during our ride back home, we reflected on Jan's warm spirit. It was such a blessing to be in her presence. This young lady did not seem to "know" she was in a wheelchair and was unable to move her legs or stretch her arms. She seemed oblivious to her condition. Or was it a condition? What would have been a "condition" to us was her reality. What she exhibited was a sense of satisfaction and joy to be able to interact with others and not be put off or feel put down. Again, truly, a vessel of honor.

It was at that exact moment that I began to thank the Lord for my ability to sit up straight, to be able to stretch out my arms and legs. To feel the joy of running (like I really can run), to feel the joy of walking the mall and not have to endure the stares of other people. This is what we take for granted. It is being made in His image that we are to receive the most joy. Not what is on the outside but the inside.

We need to change our mindset. Replace sorrys with thank yous. Instead of saying 'sorry I am late" try, thank you for waiting on me. This is the new thought I received after spending just a few minutes with Jan.

I prayed:

"Lord help me to change my mind set. Help me to recognize how blessed I am just to be in your presence. To be created in your image. Let me share your image with others, not what I see in me, but what I see in you.

Thank you, Lord, for life. And that more abundantly!

Amen

CHAPTER 5

❧

WHO AM I?

"Therefore, if any man be in Christ, he is a new creature: .."
– 2 Cor. 5:17a KJV

While shopping the other day, I stopped to admire the most exquisite mirror. The detail of the design in the wood was just unbelievable. The wood was smooth to the touch. It had a nice warm brown color. Not mahogany and not maple. Seriously, I fell in love with this piece of furniture. But that's not really what I want to share with you. I looked into the mirror at my reflection. Now in and of itself that is not unusual. But for some reason, this time, I saw more than just a natural reflection. More than just a grey-haired woman with brown eyes and a wide smile. I saw a person who is carrying a great responsibility. An individual who wears several hats. An individual who sometimes doubts and wishes she could be almost anyone else. I am sure you feel that way too at times.

Over the years, we all wear several hats. Men and women. We become somebody's wife or husband. Someone's mother or father. Someone's child or grandchild. Someone's supervisor. Someone's student, leader, pastor, teacher, doctor, lawyer or accountant. We take pride in our business endeavors. We become entrepreneurs, homeowners, business property owners, messengers, clerks, prophets, poets and writers. We wear a myriad of hats over the years. When are we going to learn who we really are? Why do we wake up each morning and say to ourselves, 'which hat am I wearing' today? Who am I today?

If I do not know who I am, in the natural, how can I ask God to bring me into his greater glory, in the spirit. I had lost my identity. I must first find myself before I can understand who God wants me to be in Him.

Take this hint, this nudge to examine yourself. Find out what you need to do to be who the Lord wants you to be. Find out who you really are. Then begin to build on the roadmap that the Lord has provided.

The next time you look in the mirror, do not focus on your outward. Look at your inward. Ask the Lord to show you yourself. Lord, where should I be. What am I suppose to be doing? Am I where I need to be in my personal life. What about my spiritual self. Show me, Lord.

Let's look at Gideon in the Book of Judges. Here in the Book of Judges, chapter 6, beginning at verse 11, we see Gideon threshing wheat by the winepress, to hide it from the Midianites. The Midianites were enemies to the children of Israel.

Gideon was called by God to perform a valiant service. In fact, the angel of the Lord said to Gideon, "The Lord is with thee, thou mighty man of valour". Judges 6:12 KJV The angel referred to Gideon as a 'mighty man of valour" but Gideon did not see himself as a warrior. Gideon had no doubts about what he saw when he looked into the mirror every morning. He saw a rough, hard himself as a thresher. He saw himself as a servant. A field worker. He never considered himself as a man of valour. Is not that what we say?

Gideon immediately began to make excuses. Did I hear the angel correctly? Gideon was so unsure, that he even fleeced God. He asked God to do something that could only be performed by God. This is what we do today. We fleece God all the time. Lord if this is you, then show me this. Or do that. Why do we not just believe? We say we know Him. We say we believe, but do we?

It took God's answer to Gideon's request to do the natural impossible before Gideon was willing to accept who God said he is. Stop fleecing

God. Accept who He says you are. You are His anointed. You are His called. You are His believer. You belong to Him. You are His creation.

Each day, resolve to recognize to whom you belong. Remind yourself, "I am God's chosen. I am His beloved." I am a new creation in Christ. Whatever is old in my life is passed away. Whatever I did when I was twenty is passed away. Let me not go backward. Let me continue to move forward in Christ, Jesus. Let me shed the old and become a new creature in Him.

The way you view yourself is the way other people will view you.

God made us to be fine china. Why do we allow people to treat us like paper plates?

God guides us like he guided Gideon. He places within us all that He needs for the time that it is needed. The difference is, we do not need to fleece God to have Him prove who He says He is. We know Him and the power of His might. We know His grace. For He is omnipotent, omniscient, and omnipresent. Gideon did not have confidence in what God was calling him to do. He was not a warrior, he thought. Little did he know, he was a warrior.

When we lose sight of who we are in Christ. We allow everyone to step on us. To kick us out of place. To pile all of their burdens and backpacks on us. All because we fail to trust the Word of God and who He says we are. It is important to remember that no matter what happens in our lives we are His children and the sheep of His pasture.

Walk in what God has for you today. Be new wine in new wineskins. Accept what God has for you. Don't just hear His voice; really listen to what He is saying. Harden not your heart. If He said go, then go. Trust Him.

So, the next time you look in a mirror see yourself as you really are. God's chosen. God's anointed. You are china. Fine china. You should be treated as fine china.

Gideon was fine china that had been stored away. But it was now time to bring out the fine china. God has a way of keeping His china for the best events. He hides His china in cabinets, cleaned and waiting for use. Gideon was working, threshing the wheat. When God called a person, look at Abraham, Moses, David, Elisha., to name just a few. Look at John, Matthew, Mark, Luke, Paul and Peter that Jesus chose. They were all working.

When they looked in the mirror in that fateful day of being called, no doubt they each saw themselves not as God saw them but as other people saw them or treated them. Mama, Grandmother, Aunt, Niece, Teacher, Friend, Pastor, Counselor, Attorney, Nurse, Doctor, Clerk, Scientist, Coach. You name it, that's who you are to someone. Maybe many some ones.

Be willing to allow the Lord to look closely into your heart. Be willing to accept that we all become someone different to others. But never forget that you are a child of the King. King Jesus.

CHAPTER 6

IT'S A MIND THING

What consumes your mind, controls your life.
– Raymond Williams

You have heard it said, 'the devil is after your mind'. Well, guess what, it's true.

James, a servant of God and of the Lord, Jesus Christ, wrote a letter to the twelve tribes who were scattered around the nation. He offered instruction and words of encouragement, as reflected in the book entitled James in the New Testament. I want to focus your mind on a particular scripture, James 1:8 "A double minded man is unstable in all his ways." (KJV) The Passion Translation puts it this way, *"When you are half-hearted and wavering it leaves you unstable. Restless or disengaged. Noncommittal. Can you really expect to receive anything from the Lord when you're in that condition.?"*

In all of my efforts to understand, to reach out to walk in and be surrounded by the presence of the Lord; I now understand why it seemed to be eluding me. My mind was not stable. I had to come to the realization that I could not have the world and Christ at the same time. I had to make a choice. The Lord led me to Deuteronomy, chapter 30, verse 19. It was if He was speaking directly in my ear. *"I call heaven and earth to record this day against you, that I have set before you life and death, blessing and cursing: therefore choose life, that both thou and thy seed may live:"* (KJV)

I had to choose one or the other. Yes, we live in this world but we do not have to be of this world. I had to exercise the faith that I said I had in Jesus. I had to walk in what I believed. That Jesus is Lord and He is the Lord of my life. My Savior. Our Savior.

A person with a divided allegiance cannot be trusted. In other words, he or she is otherwise called a spy. Our enemy, the devil, is after our minds. If he can get us to think that God does not exist; that Jesus is not our key to life; that we do not need to pray; to gather together in unity as a group of believers; that we are alone; that the God we have been praying to and reading about is just not as strong as we are led to believe.

It is this type of thinking that the devil, the enemy uses to keep us bound. He messes with our minds. So how do we move forward?

Jesus said, "But seek first his kingdom and His righteousness, and all these things will be given to you. Therefore, do not worry about tomorrow, for tomorrow will worry about itself. Each day has enough trouble on its own. " St. Matt. 6:33-34 NIV

Faith requires us to step out. Faith by simple definition means, moving by what we have trust in, not what we see with our physical sight. The Passion Translation of the Bible, quoted above, provides us with this simple revelation. We hope for that which we cannot see, but faith brings what we cannot see into manifestation, or reality. I am not saying that just because we speak it, it appears. Whatever "it" is. I am saying that if we have enough faith to believe that "it" can happen, "it" can become. For it is by the perseverance of our faith that we are successful.

Every journey, no matter how long it may be, begins with a single step. Christ took the ultimate step for us. Now it is our turn to take a step not only for ourselves but also for others by accepting Jesus as our Lord and Saviour so that many lives may be in His. This is my journey. This is my choice. This is what single mindedness will bring us to. Our journey. Our purpose.

My faith was being tested even as I wrote this chapter. I felt misunderstood. I felt unnecessarily pressured. Intimidated, harassed, mentally anguished, regretful, attacked. All of these feelings flooded over me. I was being challenged because I made a decision to move forward with what I heard the Lord say. When I gave the directive to the people in the congregation there were a lot of oohs and aahs. There was a very strong, "Are you sure you heard the Lord correctly"? Yes, we do sometimes question our own selves as to what we are hearing. I had gone back to the Lord. I know why they were feeling stumped or amazed. It even sounded strange to me.

I had no specific long-term, formal, upbringing in church other than to attend when my grandmother went to the church on the corner. Or when I turned eight and started attending the big Catholic church. Attending a church and understanding what it means to be a part of the church I now know to be completely different.

I was not ready for real church when we moved to Northeast. I was still grappling with certain passages of scripture. Trying to understand what I was supposed to know that would ease my fears. Trying to sort out what's right and what's wrong. My soul was so very hungry. I had lots and lots of questions. Yet, I was not ready for what I received. There was so much talk about what we could or could not wear. You know what I mean. We were told it was a sin to wear red shoes or shoes with the toes cut out. No hot combing the hair. No perms. Girls don't wear pants or makeup. No gym classes for me. No swimsuits.

No. No. No. It did not matter what it was if it was fun, the answer was no. Services were held all day on Sunday; Wednesday and Friday nights services were also mandatory. Bible study on Tuesdays and choir rehearsal of Thursdays. There was no time for anything else. If it was not "church" it was not worth getting involved; it was of this world. That is what we were told. Was this what we had to look forward to? When these thoughts came across my mind, I felt guilty. Was God going to punish me. Would I see heaven in peace?

I love Apostle Paul. He said, "*When I was a child, I spoke as a child, I understood as a child, I thought as a child: but when I became a man, I put away childish things.*" 1 Corinthians *13:11* As I read and re-read over this passage of scripture, the treasure trove of knowledge and wisdom, I knew I had made the right choice. I chose to accept Christ as my personal Savior. For Him. For the saving of my soul and the souls of others.

I took the Word of the Lord very seriously. I tried to put into practice everything that I read. Everything that I was being taught. As I continued to grow in the grace and the Word of the Lord, my understanding became clearer.

Remember Jeremiah 2:13, "For my people have committed two evils: They have forsaken Me, the fountain of living waters, and hewn themselves cisterns-broken cisterns that can hold no water. "Many times, in our lives, we learn things when we are young that do not carry over well into our adult life. This was one of those things. I believe what the Lord is saying here is, that we should not throw away what we were once taught as being incorrect. But to remember that we were only taught what was taught to our teachers at that time. For a teach can only teach what they know. But now that we have the ability to read, write and understand, for ourselves, and the wisdom to ask the Holy Spirit for an interpretation that we can handle, we re-read the same word with a different meaning or understanding; a different view point. We are encouraged to search the scriptures to seek wisdom from God. As we move forward with that practice, as we open ourselves up to receive more and He know that we can be trusted with more, our understanding of His word grows.

What is a cistern? The word cistern is taken from the Latin cisterna, which means "box"; from the Greek word that means basket. They are often built to catch and store rainwater. They are distinguished from wells by their waterproof linings. When we as human beings build our own boxes, our own cisterns they are subject to leak. Thereby rending them useless. For they hold nothing. When we allow God to build the cistern it will never leak.

What does this have to do with my decision and the subsequent experiences that I shared. Just this, the fact that we have been holding on to what we heard others say without seeking the truth through the Word of God. We have been using cisterns (boxes) built by man and not God. Therefore, there has been much leaking of truth; much leaking of spirit; much leaking of peace. Much leaking of understanding.

It would be unfair to say that we were deliberately being taught a lie. For nothing is a lie if it is all you know. It is not until new information, new thoughts, new directions have been introduced that we find that what we know is not all there is to know; or to experience or to understand. I believe this is why Paul encouraged Timothy to be *diligent in studying; to present yourself approved to God, a worker who does not need to be ashamed, rightly dividing the word of truth.* 2 Timothy 2:15. (KJV) I wanted to learn how to rightly divide the word of truth. I wanted so desperately to be a vessel of honor. So I endured. I took in every word.

I had not, nor have I now arrived, but like the Apostle Paul, "*I press toward the mark of the prize of the higher calling, in Christ Jesus*". Philippians 3:14 KJV

Choices are important. Right choices are even better. I was glad that I had finally made up my mind to fully serve the Lord. I have not regretted it. Each day's experiences brings us closer and closer to where we need to be. Each verse of scripture we read, we understand provides more insight, more knowledge, more wisdom, more revelation for the purposes for which God has created us. Each step brings a new grace, new dimensions, and, yes, new distractions. I must inform you that there will be distractions because you need to be ready.

Every new task seems overwhelming. Things are not always as they seem. Nothing is as simplistic as it may appear. Yes, God is the righteous judge. Yes, God is our keeper and provider. Yes, God cares about us so much so that He gave his only begotten Son who gave up His own life for us. But it is not as simple as it may seem.

The congregation accepted the direction that was provided. They trusted the word that the Lord had given. We were blessed by it. Truly blessed. They were delighted. More importantly, they expressed a new awareness and eagerness to worship the Lord in spirit and in truth.

CHAPTER 7

DECISIONS, DECISIONS

"Multitudes, multitudes in the valley of decision!"
– Joel 3:14 KJV

Decisions, decisions, decisions. Everyday we make decisions. What to wear? What to eat? How am I supposed to think? Does she or he really care? What did they mean by that word? Why did'nt he or she speak to me? Is this what God wants me to do? How do I know? What do I want to do with my future? Do I even have a future?

The word decision means a conclusion or resolution reached after consideration; the action or process of deciding something or of resolving a question; a formal judgment. The American Heritage Dictionary of the English Language, New College Edition,1976 p.342

Why did I give you the definition? Because I want to be sure we are on the same page. We are not yet talking about a formal judgment such as a judicial decision handed down by a judge. Although we could discuss it. But not yet.

I do want to talk about the resolution reached after consideration, definition. Let us begin here.

Every good and perfect gift comes from God. We came from God. God made a perfect man and a perfect woman. Adam and Eve. But

Adam and Eve were given choices. They, too, had to make a decision. They had freedoms to enjoy, dress, and keep the Garden of Eden but there were still choices to make. They were told they could eat from every tree in the Garden but one. Adam knew the Word of the Lord. We assume he gave that word to his wife. She was deceived by the serpent who was sly and proceeded to distract her with words that were almost correct. She allowed her flesh to take over. She made the decision to eat from the forbidden tree. She then gave that forbidden fruit to her husband, Adam, and the scripture said, ***"he did eat also"***. As soon as he ate, the scripture says, ***"And Adam heard the voice of God walking...."***. Genesis 3:8 KJV Wow, what a word.

Can you imagine hearing the voice of God walking? Do voices even walk? Maybe it was the voice of God I heard walking when I attended the service with Dr. Twiggs. Decisions will always be around. We make decisions every day. Are the decisions you make, made with God's will in mind or yours?

We must take decisions one step at a time. When we look over the horizon we become overwhelmed by the vastness of space between where we are and where we need to go. It appears to be an eternity. Something that will never happen. It will take too long; cost too much. Sometimes it causes us to hold back on making a decision that will benefit us because we are scared of the distance we need to go or the direction is not clear; we are afraid that we will be wrong; we become obsessed over being liked rather than being obedient.

Tony Robbins, an American author and life coach guru, is quoted, as saying, ***"A real decision is measured by the fact that you've taken a new action. If there's no action, you haven't truly decided."*** Everydaypowerblog.com

How can we say we have changed if there is no fruit to reflect it. For isn't the tree known by its fruit? Was not the fig tree cursed because it bore blooms without fruit? We may act like there has been a change. We change our clothes, but do we change our mindset? We follow what is put in front of us but what happens to our thoughts?

If we continue to do what we have always done, we will get what we have always gotten.

For the Lord did give us all great minds with which to think. In fact, Paul encouraged the Philippian church members that when things are not going well, when things are questionable; when things get out of hand, he said, ***"Finally, brethren, whasotever things are true, whatsoever things are noble, whatsoever things are just, whatsoever things are pure, whatsoever things are lovely, whasotever things are of good report, if there is any virtue and if there is anything praiseworthy—meditate on these things."*** Philippians 4:8

May I suggest we try using Paul's suggestions when we are thinking about the issues of life; maybe if we asked ourselves these questions before we made a final decision, so many of our decisions would not be regretted or regrettable. I find that when I use these helpful thoughts, I make fewer bad decisions; fewer questionable decisions; fewer decisions that I need to repent for.

Decisions can either be in words or actions. Interestingly enough, our words and our behaviors are results of decisions. Either rightly or wrongly, they say a lot about how we think and what we think about. They are the result of decisions that have already been made in our minds yet not spoken or acted on. We are decision-making machines. We must learn how to become difference-making machines. Impacting and influencing positively.

What is true is found in God (2 Timothy 2:25), in Christ (Ephesians 4:20, 21), In The Holy Spirit (St. John 16:13), and in God's Word (St. John 17:17). One translation of the scripture uses the term "noble" instead of "lovely". The Greek term "noble" means "worthy of respect." If we make noble decisions, then we are encouraged to make decisions that would be worthy of respect. Every opportunity to make a choice requires sincere thought. For whatever decision we make, there is an expected outcome. I believe it was the wisdom that Paul provided through the Holy Ghost, that we "think on these things".

Decisions made in abstract; made without considering the after affects can be detrimental to many. We must remember that in whatever state we find ourselves we must consider our actions are not solely affecting us.

What does this discussion of decisions mean in relation to becoming a vessel of honor? What does my decision to not drink soda mean to the body of Christ. Well, let's look at that. In and of itself, drinking soda is not a sin. However, if I consume too many sodas, I can damage my body. This body, that the Lord has given me, this body that was designed to be used by God and, in fact, was the first vessel (not mine) God breathe his breath into. This body becomes diseased and weakened. Illnesses such as high blood pressure, diabetes, low calcium which results in easily broken bones, among other things that excessive sugar may cause. If the body has been weakened by our own hand, how can it be a solid vessel for use. Is it not cracked and marred. Not by His hand but ours.

Yes, we can still be used by the Lord but we certainly will not have the energy, stamina or diligence to go forward. To stand when the going gets tough. This was my decision to not put unnecessary damage on the vessel to be used; the vessel that is to house the Holy Spirit, the Comforter. I believe that when I made that decision I made it with the thought that I would be deliberately causing damage to the vessel that the Lord made for long term use.

This decision was my decision. I believe that we are to take serious stock in what we put on, what we put in and what comes out (speaking) of the vessel if we are to be honorable to the Lord.

I have heard people say, don't go back over your past. I was warned that when we look over our past, our minds tend to revert backward. Some have even fallen into depression. However, in reality, it is our past that gives us perspective. We need to understand why we make the decisions we make. It is this understanding that helps us to be able to move forward to who we are to become. If our past does not serve us for betterment, then it becomes a hinderance to our future growth.

There are many times in our lives that we feel we are constantly going through the same trials, the same temptations all the time. I compare it to the children of Israel going through the wilderness for forty years; passing the same tree, year after year, after year.

Sometimes in life, situations will repeat themselves until you learn your lesson. Obviously, the children of Israel had not learned their lesson. It took them years to realize their decision to leave Egypt and follow Moses to the Promised Land was worth their struggle. However, I believe it was only a struggle because they had not learned it was their mindset, their decision to not be grateful for what they had received from the Lord God that caused them to take so long to go through.

We must learn to be grateful. I believe that is the first step toward the threshold into the greater glory of God. For the word of God reminds us that **"without faith it is impossible to please the Lord."** Heb. 11:6 KJV

For what good is being sanctified, being set apart for His use if we really cannot be used by Him because we have not fully surrendered this vessel for His full use? Yes, God can use us in whatever state He knows we are in. If we look back through scripture, He used Abraham who was a drunkard. He used Moses who was a murderer. He used David who committed adultery and who was a murder. Remember, David conspired to have the husband of his lover killed in battle to try to cover up his sin. Yet, God used him, in a mighty way. God used a harlot to save the prophet. God does use us even in our defective state. However, he would prefer that we strive daily to "press toward the mark for the prize of the high calling of God in Christ Jesus." Phil. 3:14 We are encouraged to be holy, to live holy, even as our Father which is in heaven, is holy.

CHAPTER 8

SERVANTHOOD

"Jesus answered, Nicodemus, listen to this eternal truth: Before a person can perceive God's kingdom realm, they must first experience a rebirth."

– St. John 3:3 TPT

We are taught, **"[T]hat, if you confess with your mouth, the Lord Jesus and believe in your heart that God has raised Him from the dead, you will be saved."** Romans 10:9 KJV But is that all to it? The scripture goes on in verse ten, " **For with the heart one believes unto righteousness, and with the mouth, confession is made unto salvation.**"

Is there something missing? Is it just that simple? Nicodemus was a prominent religious leader among the Jews. He was a part of the sect called the Pharisees and a member of the Jewish ruling council. Nicodemus was a respected teacher in Israel. Even with all of his statute in society, Nicodemus came to Jesus, discreetly, at night. He did not want his fellow companions to see him approach Jesus, this Nazarite; this proponent of a gospel that was in direct opposite to what he had been taught. This gospel, this word that he had heard being touted from this very plain, carpenter, had struck a nerve in him. This word caused Nicodemus to think about his own personal life and how he was living it.

Nicodemus acknowledged Jesus as "Master". While Nicodemus may have been embarrassed to met with Jesus during the day because of his position, He honored him at this late hour of the night. Acknowledging that He (Jesus) performed miraculous signs and that no one could do such things without God's power is with him.

Jesus took the opportunity to inform Nicodemus that if he wished to follow Him, he (Nicodemus) must experience a rebirth. Of course, Nicodemus had no idea what Jesus was referring to. For he said, how can I be reborn of my mother. I am already old. Isn't that how we see the Word, sometimes when we do not understand the meaning of what is being said. Is not this how we react when we have joined the church, accepted Christ (following the Romans scripture) and yet, we are told there is more?

Jesus had to lay it out plainly. He said, **" I speak an eternal truth: Unless you are born of water and Spirit, you will never enter God's kingdom realm. "** St. John 3: 5 KJV

How can this be, you say? Jesus began to explain to Nicodemus by breaking down the parable in a simpler, more natural term and yet, Nicodemus had trouble believing. Jesus then referenced Moses' lifting up the replica of the serpent on a pole for the people to see and be healed. He then said, **"'so the Son of Man is ready to be lifted up so that those who truly believe in him will not perish but be given eternal life."** St. John 3:14-16 KJV

Picture this. You have been a member of a church or fellowship (as they are now called), for six years. You're sitting in the service enjoying the move of God and suddenly, your mind says, "I can do that. "I can deliver the word of the Lord, like that person". Really, now. Yes, you may be able to quote a few scriptures. Yes, you may be able to speak in tongues. Yes, you may be able to offer a prayer or word of encouragement. But are you really ready to be used by the Lord?

The operative issue is, being 'used' by Him and for Him rather than performing a service in our own ability. All of us perform services every day. We go to our respective places of employment. We go to school, be it high school or college. We work full-time and part-time jobs. These are services.

One definition of the term service is, an action of helping or doing something for someone. If you notice the examples above, they all involve performing a work for someone.

The definition of use, "to take, hold, or deploy (something) as a means of accomplishing a purpose or achieving a result." Let me take this opportunity to explain what I mean here. If I want to be of service to the Lord, then I assume that I am worthy. What I fail to realize is that in and of myself, I am not worthy to be of service. I must present myself, humbly before my God, my Lord and Saviour, who is gracious enough to grant me the strength, the wisdom and the ability to be of use to him. In other words, if I believe I am able to accomplish a task on my own ability, then I have already failed. However, if I admit that it is only by His mercy and His grace that I can be used, He will grant me the wisdom, skills and abilities necessary to accomplish the task at hand.

Maybe you say, this is a play on words. Well, I guess it depends on how you look at it. But I certainly do not want to be turned away from the opportunity to perform a task that He may need. It is my desire to always be available for His use. Like the vessels at the wedding supper that were used by Jesus.

Someone said, 'the eye sees only what the mind is prepared to comprehend'. I do not know who said this but it certainly has turned out to be a true comment. For as long as we can see a thing, our minds accept it. Yet, what happens to our faith. What happens when we must walk by faith.

Every morning when we awaken, we ask the Lord, (I hope) what can I do for you today? How can I help someone find their way to you. How can I let my light shine so that men may see your good works?

Lord, we pray. Make me an instrument for your service. I know you have uttered those words from time to time. So have I. And not so long ago. I hear testimonies from many different people who say, "I want to preach the gospel". "I want to serve as a missionary and go to other countries to help others." "I want to reach out to the poor." I want to aid those who are mentally challenged". "I want to build homes for the elderly." There are many needs. Many dreams, many ways in which to serve. Many opportunities to be of service but are we truly ready?

We must see it before we see it. Yes, we must see the thing in our spirit before we see it in the natural. What is a dream, a vision a desire for the future without faith? The Apostle Paul encouraged the saints in his letter to the church in Rome, but what saith it? The word is nigh thee, even in thy mouth, and in thy heart: that is, the word of faith, which we preach. Rom. 10:8 Paul was taking about salvation, the acceptance of Jesus as their Lord, but he was also encouraging them to believe the word of the Lord that had been given that they might stay faithful and encouraging one another.

How can I know that I am ready to be used if I am never tried? Why must we wait to be tried before we move out to do a work for the Lord? Is there some way I can exercise my faith without being tried? How do you know you understand long division without the test. Yes, you sat in elementary school for weeks learning it. There were many practice exercises and much homework. However, it was not until we had the real examination in long division that we knew 'for real' if we understood the process.

Just as we have lessons and tests in school, we have lessons and tests in our spiritual walk. Everyone wants to be used by God. I accept that. But when test day comes, we must ask ourselves, 'am I ready'?

1 Peter 1:7, " **That the trial of your faith, being much more precious than of gold that perisheth, though it be tried with fire, might be found unto praise and honor and glory at the appearing of Jesus Christ."** KJV

This is a reminder that our faith will be tried. However, it also reminds us that it is necessary that our faith be tried because it is more precious than gold that we might be found unto praise and honor and that our lives glorify Jesus, the Christ. Let us not take our testing, our trials lightly. For, it is through the trial that we learn to be grateful. It is through them that we learn to stay humble before our God. It is through them that we learn to love the Word of God, as it is His Word that provides our strength. It is His Word that gives us comfort. It is His Word that give us joy. It is His Word that lasts forever.

The Prophet Isaiah was told by God to "Cry" to the people. He asked, "What shall I cry? All flesh is grass, and all the goodliness thereof is as the flower of the field: The grass withered, the flower fadeth: because the spirit of the Lord bloweth upon it surely the people is grass. The grass withereth, the flower fadeth: but the word of our God shall stand for ever." Isaiah 40:6-8 KJV

Isaiah reminds us that we are like grass, we wither in the heat, we struggle in the cold but we are rejuvenated only when the warmth of the Word of God has visited us and dwells inside. Like the grass that grows like wildfire after a rain. It is His rain that we need. His water. His Word. The Word that brings life and hope and love.

During the tough times of life, we need something that will last. Something that will not fail. That 'something' is the Word of God. It will not fail. It will never fail us. It is the only truth that we can depend on. As Isaiah said, the word of God shall stand for ever.

CHAPTER 9

BECOME AN INFLUENCER

Teaching others has value.

When you're gone, what will people remember you for? What legacy will you leave? Will it be something someone can learn from and grow to become successful or will it be something that leaves others to wonder what you did with your life?

I want to be an influencer for good, for great, for peace. I had to ask myself the same question. I want to be an influencer. I want others to see Christ in my life. I asked myself, what can I offer mankind that will better their lives? How can I help bring them to Jesus?

Today was a good day. Our new series in Bible study was about being an influencer for good; for great; for peace. We can either be an influencer for good or for bad. We want our effect on people to be for the best; to encourage betterment. Being an influencer is real work. Being an influencer means our faith will be tried.

Take Moses, for example. He was born into slavery yet, he became a strong influencer for God. He became a great leader. The scripture tells us that he was a goodly child. The Lord used his enemy's daughter to hide him in plain sight. Right under Pharoah's nose-- in his own house. It is amazing that God hid Moses right in the middle of his enemy's face. God allowed Moses to grow up with the pleasures of the world. Decadence, money, slaves, the best foods. Moses was in Pharoah's household for forty years. Then, after he comes to himself, he is sent out to the dessert to live for another forty years. No rich foods, no decadence, no opulence. Just survival. What was God's point? But that is another story. God has truly got a sense of humor.

Although Moses was born to a Hebrew slave, he grew up in the palace and was treated as one of the king's family. However, God used Moses to see how the Hebrews were being treated. With such negativity. Such maliciousness. Moses saw one of the Hebrews being beaten by an Egyptian taskmaster. The scripture says, **"And he looked this way and that way, and when he saw that there was no man, he slew the Egyptian, and hid him in the sand."** Exodus 2:12 KJV Isn't it ironic that two Hebrews who were fighting amongst each other the next day, said to Moses, **"will you smite us also?"** Exodus 2:13 KJV. This coming attitude from the same group of individuals he was trying to help. I am sure you have experienced similar situations, or at the least, know of someone who has been in a similar situation.

Here Moses thought he was helping the Hebrews by killing an Egyptian that was beating one of their own. And yet it was that incident; that act of what Moses took for kindness, that resulted in him fleeing for his life because he had been seen committing a murder. Sometimes God just works in unusual ways. God used this opportunity to bring Himself to Moses' attention. Sometimes what we take for good turns out differently from what we had expected. Sometimes our helping someone else turns out to ultimately help us to make clearer decisions for our own lives.

This was the start of Moses' call to the Lord. There is always a beginning before the beginning. God was setting the stage for Moses to become a believer in the "I AM". This was Moses' first lesson to becoming an influencer.

The journey to becoming an influencer takes many turns and requires much patience, much faith and much prayer. Sometimes God will take us through the long road to reach our destination before He is ready to speak to us about our purpose. Moses ran away from Egypt to save his own life. He ran to the land of Midian. Midian in Hebrew means, "place of judgment'. Surely this was not by accident. How ironic is that. Moses who was born a slave and was being served in the king's palace, as a royal, finds himself ending up in a place called judgment. What was Moses expected to learn here? Did Moses know he was being taught how to lead God's people? Of course not. And as quietly as it is kept, neither do we when we first encounter God's teaching methods.

I believe Moses' mother knew he was called to be a servant for the Lord at his birth. She knew of Pharoah's new law—to kill all the male Hebrew children that were being born at that time. It was Pharoah's deliberate effort to thwart God's plan to have a redeemer for the Hebrews. Obviously, Pharoah had no clue as to whom he was dealing. He had no clue who he was protecting in his own palace; living among his own family.

Moses' mother, had to protect her special son. She put him in a tiny reed basket on the river. God used her act of courage to place her son, the Hebrew child of his choice, in the house of Pharaoh, a house of greatness.

God had plans for this young child. He would place Moses, who would ultimately become the enemy to his now surrogate father, in the center of the hurricane to protect him and teach him until it was time for Moses to be used by God. We have similar experiences, ourselves. We just need to think about them.

God will hide us in the center of the storm to keep us safe while He prepares and proceeds to perform what He needs to perform. So as we walk through the valley of the shadow of death, the scripture says, fear no evil. God is with us. God is with you. Every step of the way. He will never leave you nor will He forsake you.

God has a very unusual sense of humor. He will allow us to go through wilderness-like conditions only to bring us out victorious so that He will get the glory and we will learn more about who He is.

The Lord teaches us when we are ready to be taught. I am a proponent of the old adage, **"when the student is ready, the teacher will come."**

Many times we just do not realize that everything that happens to us; everything that we experience, both good and bad, teaches us lessons. Lessons about ourselves, about God, about Jesus, and our relationship to others.

Moses became the son-in-law to Reuel (Jethro) and learned how to be an excellent shepherd. Years later, the king of Egypt died. The Israelites were groaning beneath their burdens. They were deep in slavery. They wept before the Lord. He heard their cries and remembered his promise to Abraham, Isaac and Jacob. What was this promise? To bring the descendants back into the land of Canaan. It was time for a rescue. It was time for Moses to go to work.

Have you ever had one of those days when you were minding your own business and you saw something strange? You felt a warmth come over you? You thought you saw someone, a shadow from a plane, a bird, maybe? Maybe you felt as if someone was shadowing you. Have you ever stopped to think that it might just be one of the angels that the Lord sent to 'watch over you'? He did say he would dispatch angels to take charge over you.

Moses encountered a burning bush. Not just any burning bush. A bush that was on fire yet not consumed. Look for your burning bush. Look for your attention getter from God. Surely, He has not been teaching you all this time for nothing. He has a plan for you and me. We can all be used. There is much work to be done. The harvest is plentiful but the laborers are few.

God is not hung up on degrees or certificates. While He will use individuals with degrees, He does not require individuals to have earned degrees. He is the degree Himself. He gives us the wisdom, knowledge and understanding to perform the services He requires. Think about it, the Old and New Testaments are rife with regular people who were used by God. He uses all types, sizes, colors, nationalities and socio-economic levels. God is not a respecter of persons. He used a harlot named Rahab to protect the Hebrew spies from being killed. Now, I am not advocating that you should not continue to search the scriptures, nor am I saying you should not endeavor to obtain more biblical knowledge by attending an institution of formal training, I found it to be most useful. Particularly, in today's world.

The Word of God is being challenged everyday. We who are "the called" must be ready to answer when needed and appropriate. Not for arguments sake but to explain why we believe and what we believe. Yes, there will be scars from the battle but those scars can be used to draw others to Christ.

In Japan, broken objects are often repaired with gold. The flaw is seen as a unique piece of the object's history, which adds to its beauty. Consider this when you feel broken. Consider that it is God's way of repurposing you to do His will. To show that you are still human but can be used by Him. Others will know that if you can be successful in Christ, they can be as well.

Get ready to be used by God. Get ready to be trained and exercised. Get ready to be tested. Expect the unexpected. Ask the Lord to give you an open mind to receive His teaching. To receive 'The Teacher', Paul said, we are to '**study to show ourselves approved unto God, a workman who needed not to be ashamed; rightly dividing the word of truth**'. 2 Timothy 2:15 (KJV)

Moses could not reach the head nor the heart of the Israelites without being taught by God. He had not lived their lives. He had not been treated as a slave. He had not been told when he could use the restroom, when he could eat or even when he could have a drink of water. He had not been limited in any manner. He had to come to grips with the knowledge of who he really was. No doubt he struggled with himself. Moses had been taught how to lead by living as an Egyptian. However, it was now time to learn how to lead a group of people; a nation that had been called and set aside by God. He had to be taught patience because truly the people he was about to lead sure tried his and God's patience, mightily.

Just as Moses had to be taught; had to be put back on the potter's wheel to be reshaped for the Master's use, we too, must be put back on the wheel. The scripture lets us know that when the Potter saw that the vessel was marred, he put it back on the wheel. We should count it a blessing to be placed back on the Potter's wheel to be reshaped for service. It is then and only then that we can be of full use. No leaks, no cracks, no weak areas.

Moses was broken and he had to be healed from his past. From both his real parents' legacy and Pharaoh's that had been imprinted upon him. We are the same. We have two parents; two sets of biological genes that imprint our being from the inside. Even our parent's parents, to some extent, imprint us. Then, of course, come outside influences that effect our attitudes and actions. These outside influences sometimes include, teachers, friends, acquaintances, jobs, schools, etc. So, our imprinting comes from many sources.

We must take heed to learn from our mistakes. Learn from the hurt. Learn from the past. Let it become the prologue into our future. Not to drag us back but to push us forward.

The Lord used Moses' experience with his father-in-law, herding sheep and tending fields; tilling and living off the land to prepare him for his journey to build a nation. Learning how to weather the storms of life and the changes in our environment teach us many things. For example, in the nature realm, we know that rain comes for a reason to prepare the ground to bring forth its fruit. We, as human beings, require cover (for the most part) when it rains as we do not grow as trees and grass. Although if you take a look at some of our children's clothes as they begin to grow they seem to react the same as the grass. They grow straight up.

Without rain nothing grows, learn
To embrace the storms of life. Wachabuy.com

In the spirit, we receive the Word of God and the outpouring of the Holy Spirit which helps us grow on the inside. It is the rain of heaven that brings us before the throne of God to grow in His grace. Just as the natural environment around us needs rain and sunshine, so does our spirit.

God used his creations to teach Moses how to get ready to accept his assignment to free the Israelites. It would take, a lot, for Moses to be ready. Moses spent forty years in the house of Pharoah. He also spent forty years being retrained to build a nation of people out of slaves.

Just as the Lord used Moses' father-in-law, to help him learn the basics of patience and diligence, He uses everyday life to teach us. Teaching others is important. But learning how to be taught; being willing to listen, to take instruction and criticism is the beginning of learning. Learning how to accept negativity for the sake of growth and growing in the Word and work of the Lord.

There will be rejection. That's an understatement, of course. I can imagine that Moses was frustrated after the first few times Pharoah rejected his warning. In fact, I would venture to say that the first time he was rejected by Pharoah he felt worthless. Let's look at Exodus 3:19 when God told Moses that he would come before Pharoah, deliver his message and still, Pharoah would reject him. Why, then Lord, if you already know that 'your' message is going to be rejected why do you want me to go in the first place. Yet, the Lord sent Moses back, nine more times. God's divinity was showing here. Not His sovereignty. Because He could have just wiped Pharoas out. After the tenth plague, Pharoah's heart was softened for just enough time to release the children of Israel. But then, pride and anger set in. The enemy will make you think he is gone but he continues to try until the Lord says, stop. It takes the Holy Spirit to release the hand of the enemy on your life. Remember, the devil has no more authority than what the Lord allows.

Watch the signals that you receive in life. Submit to the purpose, plan and destiny that the Lord has for you. Be willing to learn and be led by His Spirit. Philippians 4:13 says, "I can do all things through Christ which strengthens me." When the Word says, all, it means all. That nothing that is done with Him shall fail. God is not obligated to make our mistakes; our transgressions right. He is only obligated to give us the opportunity to repent and press toward the mark of the prize of the higher calling in Him.

Moses thought he had lost his value when he left Egypt. Only to discover he had found his true worth. Allow the Lord to teach you. I have a friend who had to go through a situation for ten years before she realized she still has value to God and to man. So, do not allow yourself to become dismayed, depressed and discouraged when you find yourself in the middle of a storm. The Apostle Paul reminds us,

"We are troubled on every side, yet not distressed; we are perplexed, but not in despair; Persecuted but not destroyed; Always abounding about in the body the dying of the Lord Jesus, that the life also of Jesus might be made manifest in our body." 2 Cor. 4:8-10

May I interest you in a little prayer to get you started?

Lord, I present my petition before you, this day. Give me an understanding heart. Teach me, I pray, Oh Lord. As David, your servant, said, "The meek will He guide in judgment: and the meek will He teach his way." Psalm 25:9 KJV. Help me to stay meek so that I will be able to hear the revelation of your word. Help me to stay meek so that your judgment of my actions will be received with joy. So that I will learn and turn when necessary. Why? Because I love you, Lord. I love your people. I love your walk. It is my heart's desire to do Thy Will. Help me to always remember so that your dying will not have been in vain.

Amen.

CHAPTER 10

LEAVE THE HONEY ALONE

"…and he turned aside to see the carcase of the lion: and, behold, there was a swarm of bees and honey in the carcase of the lion."

– Judges 14:8 KJV

Now this scripture has been read many times. I know you have read it or heard it read at least five times, if not fifty. Well, let me share what the Lord said to me about this scripture.

Once the Lord has allowed you to defeat your enemy, no matter how often you remember the event, do not look back. Do not eat from the same cistern that you know is contaminated. Do not be tempted to knock on the door, or call or email, or text, or facebook or twitter, the same enemy that you have just defeated. If it is supposed to be dead, let it stay dead. Stop trying to resurrect that which is dead.

Truly that thought blessed my spirit. Let us move forward to the goal that the Lord has established for us. There will be young lions, having great zeal, with loud roars and sharp claws that the enemy, the devil, will try to use to cause us harm. He will use the young lion, not something that is dried up, impotent and lackluster but something that will get your attention. Something that will cause you to stop in your tracks. Something that will be a sure distraction.

Ah, the young lion. The eager child who will try your patience. The good child who suddenly becomes the one you need to pray about. The husband that is the "love of your life"; you know the one that pledged faithfulness in sickness and in health. Yes, that one. Only to discover that at the first sign of illness, the pledge was forgotten. The wife who was there every morning preparing breakfast, loving the kids but neglecting you and the house. What happened?? Young lions have no filters. They have not yet learned to appreciate what is in front of them. it's the young lion that will cause the most pain. Young lions are immature.

I am not speaking about physical age. I am speaking about their inner spirit. The spirit of the untrained. The spirit of the unbeliever. The spirit that is lost. The spirit that is destitute. The spirit of hurt. It is the young, injured spirit that will cause the most hurt; the most destruction. Without healing….real healing through the Spirit of the Lord there can be no real deliverance.

Do not go back to the carcass. Samson knew he was not to touch the dead thing, yet alone, eat from it. Why do we get sidetracked so easily? Because our flesh is weak and the honey is sweet. Instead of reaching and leaning on our faith; instead of rehearsing the Word of God that is in our heart, we slip into our natural state of mind. Our carnal affections take over.

Samson was tempted with that which was sweet inside that which was off limits. Just because the donut is swollen does not mean it is filled with the proper filling. It's a trap.

Why are we going into this? Because if you want to be a vessel of honor; if you want to be used for the work of saving souls. If you want to cross the threshold into the greater of God; if you want to be a servant leader for Christ, we must heed his signs. His directions.

Why would we not know that the enemy is trying to distract us when he would place honey in a dead thing. God's children are not stupid. It is because our flesh is weak that the enemy or his imps will try to use whatever is allowed to distract us. If your enemy knows you like honey, he will use honey to get your attention. If he knows you like young lions, he sends young lions. Young lions filled with just enough sweetness to distract you. Touch not the unclean thing.

The common cause of disobedience is unwillingness to follow authority. Authority is not man made, even though it is carried out by man. Unwillingness to seek truth will cause and have caused many to face an eternal penalty of separation from the One who created authority. The Creator, God the Father! Authority belongs to God. Walk wisely and be obedient. Remember, the devil has to obtain permission from God to tempt you. Even with that, if you understand that the Lord has 'bragged' on you don't you think He already knows you will not give in. He knows your end from your beginning. He knows!! You can be successful in this walk with Christ only if we are willing to listen and be obedient.

Yes, we know the devil has only a partial truth to share. For he is the father of lies. He can only bring to you your history. He is not in control of your future. You are. He will try to get you to go against the truth that you have been taught. He will challenge your Word knowledge. He will try to get you to worry about things you have no control over. Worry is a waste of time. Worry will only steal your joy and keep you busy doing nothing. Satan will send whisperers to come to get you off track.

Remember, hands off! Let the cloud of whisperers move on.

Do not touch the carcase. It is a dead thing. Remember who you are. You are a Nazarite. You are a chosen one. Leave the honey alone.

CHAPTER 11

CHANGE IS AN INSIDE JOB

"I will delight myself in thy statutes: I will not forget thy word."
– Psalm 119:16 KJV

David said to the Lord, "I will delight myself in thy statutes: I will not forget thy word." In other words, David was at a crossroads. He was much like we find ourselves. When things just do not go the way we think they should. When everything fails and we feel so alone. When it seems like we have no hope. David, said, I will delight myself. How? In thy statutes. I know that my hope lies in your Word, Oh Lord. I know that my future is in Your hands. But I also recognize that there is a part that I play.

How do I get this confidence in God. The key, I have found to overcoming adversity is humility. David gave up his pride to accept the statutes of His God. The God of Abraham. The God of Isaac. The God of Jacob. David said, I will delight!. That just got me excited right there. I *will* delight.

In other words, no matter what shall take place, I will delight! Let us keep that in mind. The enemy would like us to drop our guard; revert to an old mind set that kept us down and out; remind us of all the negative things that had been said about us to throw us off guard. But remember those words, 'I will delight' myself in they statutes. We must possess an inner strength of God. Change comes from the inside.

I was standing in the lobby of a medical office building while I was awaiting the opening of another office. I happened to look up and saw several ceiling tiles dislodged or missing. I had been coming through this particular office building for years but never thought to look up at the ceiling. The building, at eye level, was always clean or being cleaned. There was never any trash on the floor, no dirt, no unemptied trash cans. It always appeared to be clean and fresh. But I never looked beyond my eye level. Why on this day?

The Lord spoke to me through this experience. He said, as long as we are looking straight ahead, as horses with eye guards, we do not see anything but what we are expected to see. Horses in the city are fitted with eye guards to keep them from being distracted as they proceed on their journey through the city. Eye guards keep the horse from getting skittish or distracted when in traffic. It is the same here. The Lord was saying I have placed eye guards on you so that you do not become distracted. For just as you were stopped in your tracks and stood looking up at the broken ceiling, you can be distracted from your mission.

We must stay focused on the mission. There will be many distractions. But the Lord will keep us, if we want to be kept.

Had you seen the broken or missing tiles before you would have been afraid. I wanted to show you how I covered you all this time. Allowing you to go about your usual appointments and not worring about being hurt. You put your trust in me and I covered you.

God is not a father that would lead his children into temptation or into danger. For the scripture lets us know that He does not tempt us. "Let no man say when he is tempted, I am tempted of God: for God cannot be tempted with evil, neither tempteth he any man: But every man is tempted, when is drawn away of his own lust, and enticed." Jas. 1:13-14

God is not a father that would allow burdens to be placed on His children that they cannot handle. If we encounter burdens that are too heavy for us to handle, David gave us hope in Psalm 55, verse 22, "Cast thy burden upon the Lord, and he shall sustain thee: he shall never suffer the righteous to be moved." KJV For the scripture reminds us, as well, that Jesus said, "For my yoke is easy, and my burden is light." St. Matt. 11:30 KJV

In fact, the Apostle Paul reminds us in 1 Corinthians chapter 10 verse 13, "There has no temptation taken you but such as is common to man" which refers to the limitation God has placed on Satan as it relates to us. So I encourage you to not worry about the outside, remember that the Spirit of God is on our inside and it is His Spirit that keeps us covered, keeps us calm, keeps us safe.

Let's face it, many of our issues, our burdens are self-inflicted. They come as a result of our own decisions. Not putting God first but moving on our own impulse; moving on emotion and not acknowledging the facts of the situation. One writer puts it this way, 'when instruction is given, rebellion always rises up against it.' Rebellion creates burden. For the scripture says, 'rebellion is as the sin of witchcraft...' 1 Sam. 15:23 KJV

Our Father, our Savior, our Protector invites us to place our burdens at His feet. So why would He allow us to be in situations that we cannot overcome? For with Him, all things are possible. When we are ready to handle the next level, He will show it to us.

I do believe He was letting me know that I had moved up in the Spirit realm. That He had allowed me to take another step toward the next threshold to the greater glory in Him.

I pondered this revelation for quite sometime. When I think of the many years I had been walking through this building and never once looked up at the ceiling but straight ahead. I never noticed what was "broken" in the building.

Would I have been able to handle it had I seen this brokenness before? Would I have been as faithful to continue to walk through this building recognizing that it was possibly unsafe? Truly the Lord has a way of teaching us, as we are ready to be taught. As we become able to accept His Word and His direction. God has an uncanny way of getting our attention. Of bringing us to a realization of where we are in our own relationship with Him so that we may be of use for His work.

There are many decisions that must be made. There are experiences that must be encountered. There are trials that must be endured. There are revelations that must be revealed. Are you ready to cross over the threshold to the greater glory in God?

Change is an inside job. I was reminded of that when I was reading an advertisement about liposuction, of all things. This advertisement was offered by a new medical group in our area. They boasted about their process of pulling the stomach muscles and the hip muscles together to create a slimmer abdomen area. They also mentioned the suctioning of fat from the lower abdomen, hips and thighs for a cleaner more even appearance. While the cutting away of the excess fat and tissue; the stretching of the inside muscles and attaching them from front to rear does not sound too appealing, the after affects appear to be worth the pain, discomfort and cost. God offers us liposuction every day. Every time we hear His Word of deliverance, His Word of hope, the process of liposuction begins. Take Him up on His Word. Let Him help you with your excess baggage. Let Him help you get rid of 'the weight and the sin that so easily beset you'.

Are you willing to go through a liposuction and restructuring of the inside muscles to allow the Lord to reshape you for greater works. Are you willing to take the extra step so that you will be able to handle more of His anointing and power? Can He reshape you for better use to Him or are we only going to allow Him to reshape us for our own glory and not His? Are we not willing to go through some minor discomforts, give up a few earthly pleasures if it means someone will accept Christ as their personal Savior? This lesson will teach us much about being reshaped for His use. Reshaped so He gets the glory.

As if this revelation was not enough, the Lord took me on yet another journey. This one was more personal. I was in the waiting room being prepared to undergo a planned operation. I was escorted into a private preparation room. Again, my mind was taken to the voice of the Lord. God has a preparation room set up and assigned just for you. It is in this room that He prepares his servants (dispatches his angels) to take charge over us. It is not God's will that we be embarrassed. God offers us an opportunity to come to Him and repent. He offers us a new way of life.

The reviewing nurse went over my general medical history that would enable the anesthesiologist to provide proper sedation to handle the pain or discomfort that is expected during surgery. I looked at the reviewing nurse as the evangelist who reviews your history and prepares you for the offer of acceptance of Christ. The first person who introduces you to the process of salvation.

Then the anesthesiologist came in. She proceeded to ask questions about medications that I may be taking and whether or not I had any prior surgeries. Depending upon the answer she then asked if I had had any problems with anesthesia in the past. I then asked about the different types of sedation. I did not want to be put completely out. I looked at this person as a possible prophet who was there to help me transition through this invasive process. It is the prophet that the Lord uses to help us see our direction until we are able to see it ourselves through the eyes of God.

What is the sedation? Sedation is the administering of a drug to produce a state of calm or sleep. This process is used to keep the patient comfortable during a process of cutting away and cleaning out. It allows the doctor to perform the necessary procedures to be able to allow the body to be refreshed and heal properly without the patient having to be awake and feeling everything that is being performed. Sedation, the Lord said, is His Word. It is accepting the Word, which is Christ, and allowing that Word to go through our nervous system to place us in a state of calm. It is that Word that will allow us to handle the vicissitudes of life. Sedation comes in different levels. There is twilight and general anesthesia. Whatever level we need is what the Lord uses to help us face the transitions necessary to reach our goal of getting into the greater glory.

Then the surgeon comes in and goes over all of what the other two individuals have gone over and marks the spots when the surgical incisions will be made; explaining everything as he continues. Allowing for questions, so that we fully understand the commitment we are making. The surgeon is the pastor who provides the shepherding for us. It is that person who takes the time to provide us with an understanding of the Word of God and helps us to learn how to accept and exercise our faith in that Word. It is that person who provides the comfort during the bad times, the aches and the pains; the doubts and the fears. God has provided everything that we need to help with the separation of sin from our lives.

Sometimes the physician will prescribe an antibiotic prior to surgery so that we get a head start to prevent infection. As we continue to learn the Word of God we take in the proper antibiotics that will help us stay healthy after the procedure. As we begin to let go of our sins in the natural, we accept more of Christ in the spirit. Remember, if the house is swept clean and garnished, and there is no antibiotic to keep the germs at bay, the germs return with a vengeance. As the Apostle Paul reminded Timothy, to "study to show himself approved unto God, a workman who needeth not to be ashamed, rightly dividing the word of truth." 2 Tim. 2:15 KJV We are to heed this instruction with all diligence.

It is the Word of God that becomes our antibiotic in the form of Jesus. A most powerful antibiotic that will kill the most resistant of germs. For Jesus is the balm in Gilead. It was His blood that was shed for us. It is truly the most valuable weapon we have to defeating the enemy who continues, day-after-day, to try to defeat us and keep us from moving toward the perfect will of God.

Just as we prepare our homes and gardens to withstand and/or prevent being invaded by the tiny enemies that will eat away the flowers, the fruit and the trees, the wood in our homes; we must prepare our hearts, likewise. For the natural we use companies like Terminix for pest control. For our spirit, we use the power of the Holy Ghost.

When the pastor (represented by the surgeon) comes in and provides the comforting Word of the Lord as Shepherd and caretaker of the sheep (which is us), she or he, as the case may be, provides the spiritual direction for what is needed before going before the Lord. It is that person that gives us the direction that the procedure will take. It is that person that provides the explanation of what will happen if we accept the process and continue on. It is that person that helps us by showing what needs to be cut away and assists with understanding the healing process. This is the person we look to for words of encouragement during times of stress and pain.

As we grow stronger in our relationship with the Word of God and our faith in Christ grows, our trials and tests grow, as well. The word of the Lord puts it this way, "to much is given, much is required". St. Luke 12:48b (KJV) As we move forward to performing His will in our lives, the closer we get to each threshold of greater glory, the less weight we can carry. We must strip away any excess baggage. This is where the surgeon comes in.

The Holy Spirit who will equip us for real service. First, the surgeon outlines where He will be cutting. X-rays or MRIs are taken, depending upon what is needed, so that He can see the inside from the outside. Only God can reveal what is on our inside without cutting the outside. He allows his holy vision to see our future from our beginning.

All things have a season. A life span. Once God has determined that the season for sin, the season for harassment, the season for abuse is over, He then begins the process of cutting away the unnecessary, the unwanted, the unneeded, the excess fat. After removing the fat (sin) he then gently and with great skill cuts away any damaged skin and reconnects the front to the rear for better and stronger muscles. It is this Holy Spirit, this Comforter, that performs the surgery so necessary for the betterment of the warrior's body. It is the surgeon, the Holy Spirit, who is able to strengthen and stretch our muscles and their linings so that we become a real tight fighting machine. Yes, it is important to take care of the packaging (the outer body) but without taking care of the inner body, the inner mechanisms, the outer body will not function properly; it will not be able to hold up under the pressure.

Learn to accept the changes that are needed. Learn to accept the redesign of His creation. When the potter decides to put the clay back on the wheel to be reshaped, reformed, it is for His behalf so that He gets the glory.

Change must come from the inside. Ask the Lord to perform your inner changes so that you may perform the outer changes for Him. We should be grateful that God has provided this process for us. That we are in excellent hands as we proceed to move toward the greater glory in Christ, Jesus.

CHAPTER 12

WHAT ARE YOU
BUILDING

"And no man putteth new wine into old bottles: else the new
wine doth burst the bottles, and the wine is spilled, and the
bottles will be marred, but new wine must be put into new
bottles."

– St. Mark 2:22 KJV

God always wants to do new things in our lives. The question is hold
what he brings? What if God wants to give you revelation are you
building a strong devotional life? What if He wants to give you more
finances are you tithing already? God may want to experience a deeper
worship with Him. Are you listening to music that would enhance
your nearness of Him? Or that which stirs up the flesh? God may have
something ready for you but He might be waiting to see if you are
building something to hold it.

Our quoted scripture from St. Mark, chapter 2 verse 22 says it so
clearly. No one can put anything new into something old and expect
it to last. Have you ever tried patching an old sweater with a new piece
of material? Ever notice how the threads from the old sweater tend not
to adhere easily to the new material. Then, after a couple of weeks of

wearing and washing, the old material pulls away from the new. This is what Jesus is talking about. How can he pour new material in your vessel if it is old and worn? How can he patch what cannot be redeemed without remaking? Is the item too worn to be mended? Maybe it is just time to purchase a new sweater.

So the question becomes, how can I be changed into a vessel God can use. How can I be set apart for His service. And then, once I am consecrated, (which loosely means set apart) how can I maintain this new mindset?

I had someone ask me 'where do I keep what I have learned. How can I manage all of the words of wisdom, knowledge and hope so that thieves do not come and steal it. Where can I put this treasure you speak of so that my neighbors will not covet it'? Listen folks, we are not talking about a "thing" here. We are talking about our bodies becoming living vessels for the Holy Spirit.

When we accept Christ as our personal Savior, we get excited about what He is doing in our lives. We are excited because we experience something that has never happened to us. Something that we never dreamed or imagined. Something that we sometimes cannot explain. Something that changes our atmosphere, physically and spiritually. I have heard testimonies from individuals who have shared their first experience with the Holy Spirit. For example, some have experienced being told they looked different. There have been testimonies of people stating they felt differently. They caught themselves thinking differently. Even, their five senses have become keener. They saw the world in a new light.

I, personally, experienced the flowers smelling differently; the leaves on the trees looked greener. It was like just waking up to a whole new world! It was an experience that I have not witnessed since. I was excited, ecstatic, overjoyed. I have not enough words to express my exuberance. I never felt more alive.

We receive the rights and privileges that God allows but can we walk it out. That is the real question.

I need to let you know that there were times when the Lord would move and all I could do was cry. I said to myself, why am I crying? Nothing is wrong. I have no pain. No one hurt me. I would cry for days. I did not know to whom I could talk about this. I did try to talk with my, then, pastor but that individual did not know how to counsel me about it. I had no one to talk to that I felt comfortable with.

Eventually, after a few days, the crying stopped. I prayed and asked the Lord for help. He sent me Evangelist Stephanie who knew what I was experiencing. She helped me to understand more about getting closer to the Lord. Being able to accept a revelation of His word for my life that moved me into a realm of belief that I had never experienced before, nor knew existed.

I was not physically at the church when I received the Holy Spirit. I was sitting with the Evangelist and one of the Church Mothers at the home of the Evangelist while we were awaiting the next service. Suddenly, the presence of the Holy Spirit overshadowed me. I began speaking in tongues and could not stop. The Evangelist (did I tell you she is also a Prophet and now a Pastor) stood with wide eyes, smiling and said, you have a fire inside you. The Mother was smiling; looking amazed at what was happening. I still could not stop. This went on for what seemed like ten minutes. I have no clue what I was saying. It did not make sense to me. I only know that I not only felt different on the inside, I had just experienced something new.

I was a different person. A new wineskin. A new vessel. A new building. I had experienced a greater glory of God.

Let's look at Saul in 1st Samuel 10:5-7

> v. 5 "After that thou shalt come to the hill of God, where is the garrison of the Philistines: and it shall come to pass, when thou art come thither to the city, that thou shalt meet a company of Prophets coming down from the high place with a psaltery, and a tabret, and a pipe, and a harp, before them; and they shall prophesy:

v. 6 And the spirit of the Lord will come upon thee, and thou shalt prophesy with them, and shall be turned into another man.

v. 7 And let it be, when these signs are come unto thee, that thou do as occasion serve thee, that thou do as occasion serve thee; for God is with thee."

Here, Saul, who had just been installed as the first King of Israel, was informed by the Prophet Samuel, after his coronation, what he would experience. Let us look at this scripture, carefully. Notice, here that Saul was told that he would encounter a company of prophets coming down from the high place. No doubt, they had been in worship before the Lord, God as they were carrying psaltery, and a tabret (tambourine) and a pipe and a harp. These were musical instruments that were used to give God praise. Because the prophets had been in the presence of the Lord, as they passed King Saul, he too, became overshadowed with the presence of the Lord and began to prophesy with them. Look at the mighty power of God!

Saul's building, his wineskin, was affected after he had been in contact with the holy oil by the Prophet Samuel. The scripture said, "and shall be turned into another man".

The presence of the power of God changed King Saul into a vessel that the Lord could use. The Holy Spirit was a witness to what the Prophet Samuel had already told him.

There will always be an impact following an encounter with the Holy Spirit. The anointing is a residue of the glory of God. What a word! We enjoy being in the presence of the Lord in our services. But the most important thing is, are we recognizing that it is the glory of the Lord that has presented itself and leaves its residue, its power, for us to relish in. Take a look at Moses when he was with God on Mount Sinai for forty days. There was so much glory from the Lord that engulfed him that his hair on his head and his face turned white. In fact, he was so changed that he was almost unrecognizable. I submit that what has been described is the residue of the anointing (power) of God. A power that was so strong that it changed the molecular structure and aging of the thing it surrounded. Check out Exodus chapter 34 verses 31-35.

We should be like children who have been in the center of the celebration and come out having more spaghetti on us than in us. That is what the residue of the glory should be like on us. Everyone knows what was served because it shows on the outside...our clothes, our hair, our hands. Shouldn't we reflect the residue of the glory that has encamped around us? Of course!

So, ask yourself, "am I building a vessel, a building, a new wineskin that will be able to withstand the greater glory of God"? Or will I collapse under the pressure? Are others able to see what I have been eating? Is it showing?

Seek for the after affects when you spend time with the Lord. Seek for evidence that will show through your inner spirit and be reflected on your exterior. Seek the Lord so hard that His presence shows all over you. In my readings, I saw this quote, by Paulo Coelho, "The world is changed by your example not by your opinion". While I do not know Mr. Coelho, he is certainly on point. We must stop talking so much and be the example. Paul said, we are to be living epistles (letters). In other words, our lives ought to preach louder than our lips.

CHAPTER 13

PROVOKE HIS
DIVINE FAVOR

The happiest people are the givers, not the takers.

I want to challenge you here. Seek the divine favor of God. How, you say. That is what I have been seeking. I cry out to the Lord daily. Lord, help me to be in your favor. I have tried, praying; reading the Word; fasting. But your favor still seems to elude me with each grasp, each prayer. Let's examine our options here.

First things first. Let's define favor. Favor is the 'unmerited' grace of God. Unmerited. Hmm! In other words, something that has not been earned and cannot be purchased. Only God can give His grace to us. We are never too good. Never to wise. Never too clever. We cannot give enough. We cannot sing enough. We cannot pray enough. We cannot read His Word enough.

Grace makes a man function without struggle while favor makes a man receive without asking. How do we know this? Let's look at the history of the Israelites. Moses gives us a peek in Exodus 3:21, "And I will give this people favour in the sight of the Egyptians; and it shall come to pass but, when ye go, ye shall not go empty."

"And the children of Israel did according to the word of Moses; and they borrowed of the Egyptians jewels of silver, and jewels of gold and raiment: And the Lord gave the people favor in the sight of the Egyptians, so that they lent unto them such things as they required. And they spoiled the Egyptians". Ex. 12:35-36 KJV.

The scripture uses the term "spoiled". The word spoiled means "harmed in character by being treated too leniently or indulgently." The Israelites were not accustomed to having the jewelry and gold that was given to them by the Egyptians. They were slaves. They were only accustomed to working for everything. Working in the dust and the dirt for someone else, not even for themselves. Working in the mud to make bricks; even being forced to make bricks without straw. Feeding the horses of the Egyptian army before they could eat themselves. I am sure there were many other chores that they were called upon to perform. There were few luxuries for the Israelites at that time. So the writer of the Book of Exodus used the word, 'spoiled'. Such a fitting word for such a drastic change of life. Did their sudden change of circumstances really cause them to be harmed? Was it for the purpose of indulgence or was the Lord returning to them all that they lost since they were God's chosen people? To restore what the canker worm, the palmer worm had eaten?

Isn't it just possible that the Lord wanted to provide his chosen people with a new beginning just as He said He would do. He is Jehovah-Nissi (our provider). God is a God of His word. He promised to take care of the children of Israel. He promised to "save" them. To free them. He did!! Just as assuredly, He freed us from the penalty of sin by sacrificing His only begotten Son, Jesus.

God allowed circumstances to happen in their lives to provoke them; to stimulate them for their betterment. The Israelites had the option of using the circumstances of being in the wilderness and moving forward for good or bad. As we can see, they could not stay focused. Nevertheless, the Lord always provides. It is up to us to choose how we are going to use what God is giving us. Trust the Lord. Trust that He is doing everything for our best.

How Do I Provoke God's Favor?

Everything in your life is a reflection of a choice you have made. If you want a different result, you must make a different choice. So, how do we provoke God's favor?

There are several schools of thought on this. Some say, that God cannot be provoked to give his favor. Since His favor is a gift by grace. Others say, that if we seek the favor of God we will receive it. Some say, all we have to do is prayer, or ask for it. And He, God, will give us his favor. Yet, there are still a few that believe all we have to do is be obedient to the Word of God and that will provoke God's favor. Let's look at a few scriptures.

As it is written, Jacob have I loved, but Esau have I hated. What shall we say then? Is there unrighteousness with God? God forbid. For he said to Moses, I will have mercy on whom I will have mercy and I will have compassion on whom I will have compassion. So then it is not of him that willeth, or of him that runneth but of God that sheweth mercy". Rom. 9: 13-16 KJV

This scripture clearly lets us know that God shows favor upon whom He will. Without personal merit, strength, ability, or prayer life. But because He and He alone wants to. May I suggest that we look at the promises that are provided to the believer in Deuteronomy chapter 28. I believe they provide a roadmap to God's favor.

Let's look at this scripture for a moment. Because surely, scripture tells us that if we are willing and obedient, we shall eat the good of the land. Isa. 1:19. The promises of God, are clearly a statement, a declaration or assurance that if one will do a particular thing a particular thing will happen. So the promises set forth in Deuteronomy are clearly assured statements of what God will do, or allow to be performed on behalf of those who do something else. Specifically, those individuals who observe and do (*emphasis added*) all His commands. In other words, the promises are directed to a service or work that in turn receives a reward.

Look at Isaiah's words for a moment, "If ye be willing and obedient, ye shall eat the good of the land." Isa.1:19 KJV Again, this is a "quid pro quo" statement. You do something in return for something else. Yes, you be willing and obedient, and then, you shall eat the good of the land. Is this favor?? It does not sound like it.

Favor does not require a pre-happening or pre-doing of some act. Favor comes just because God wants to do something for us. We cannot earn favor. God says he will show mercy or favor upon whom he will show mercy, it is my opinion that it is not possible to provoke God's favour. It is possible to provoke and activate His promises, however.

Moses reiterated God's promises to the children of Israel in Deuteronomy chapter 28 verses 1 through 13. However, I will draw your attention to the beginning and the end of these verses. Specifically, verse 1. "And it shall come to pass, if thou shalt hearken diligently unto the voice of the Lord thy God, to observe and to do all his commandments which I command thee this day, that the Lord thy God will set thee on high above all nations of the earth: 2. And all these blessings shall come on thee, and overtake thee, if thou shalt hearken unto the voice of the Lord thy God.; v 13. And the Lord shall make thee the head, and not the tail, and thou shalt be above only, and thou shalt not be beneath ; if that thou harken unto the commandments of the Lord thy God, which I command thee this day, to observe and to do them; " KJV

If you continue to read the 28th chapter of Deuteronomy, you will also notice that all of the promised blessings are attached to obedience. If you move down to verses 15 through 68 we discover the results of disobedience. Why waste all that goodness between verse 1 and 14, which really make up more blessed promises than any of the curses in verses 15 through 68.

Favor comes without work. Without sweat. Without tears. Without justification. Promises are those actions that require a work or effort to be released. Jesus said, "Seek ye first the kingdom of God and his righteousness, and all these things shall be added unto you." St. Matt. 6:33 KJV That's favor! Obedience is better than sacrifice.

God does not want you to try harder. He wants you to trust Him deeper. Stop trying. Learn how to receive without asking. Start trusting. This will change everything.

Entering Into His Favor:

"Blessed are the merciful, for they shall obtain mercy". Matt. 5:7 – Brethren, the level of favour you enjoy is a function of the level to which you favour others. The law of seedtime and harvest controls the issue of favour. Do you want to walk in favour? Then be a person of favor.

In the book of Esther (2:21-22), Mordeci got wind of a plan to kill king Ashasuerus and leaked it, thereby sparing the king's life. A time came when Mordecai was also to be killed, but his earlier seed of favour would not allow it. See Esther 6:1- 3.5

Have you ever tried giving to release the favor of God in your life? Yes, giving. Now, I am not talking about tithes which is giving and commanded in the Old Testament and fulfilled in the New Testament by Jesus. I am talking about giving as a way of life and a show of love. From the heart. I believe that if we have a giving heart, we capture God's attention. For He honors the cheerful giver.

The movie, Pay It Forward (released October 2000) written by Leslie Dixon and directed by Mimi Leder resulted in an unprecedented wave of human kindness. Even today, there are glimpses of that human love that peeks through some of our darkest moments. For a time, the world was a better place to live. I salute the writer, the actors and the director for sharing this jewel with us. Today, that movie still results in warm feelings as it shows us a vision of what God is requiring and the results of having his loving spirit working through us as individuals and as one family.

We experienced individuals leaving unusually nice tips to waiters and waitresses just to encourage their hearts to attain their future goals or meet some important need in their lives. We experienced seeing strangers feeding the hungry and it was not even Thanksgiving or Christmas.

It is this heart of giving that will motivate God's favor.

I am encouraging you to invoke the promises of God. Kindness is free. It is one of the simplest ways we can help make the world a better place. I have seen animals exhibit more kindness to other animals than some humans exhibit toward each other. It is the kindness of one human toward another that will defeat homelessness and hunger. If we invoke the promises, by blessing others, if we observe God's laws and commands, and do them, perform, act upon them, the Lord said He will set us on high above all nations of the earth. Wow, what an invocation to enter the greater glory of our Father.

We must be like trees. Trees, in order to grow release dead leaves. It is as if the mother tree releases those that are no longer viable. Drop whatever is hindering you from receiving the favor of God. Old friends, suggestive music, certain eating places or vacation sites, movies, magazines. Anything that reminds you or takes you back to a time or place that was not good for you or the Holy Spirit.

CHAPTER 14

PRAYERS OF THE RIGHTEOUS

"What is man that you are mindful of him, the son of man that you care for him? You made him a little lower than the angels. You crowned them like kings and queens with glory and magnificence. You have delegated to them mastery over all you have made, making everything subservient to their authority, placing earth itself under the feet of your image-bearers."

– Psalm 8: 4-6

What's With This Prayer Thing?

When I asked the question during a Bible study class, is it possible to provoke the favor of God, many people said, yes. By praying. Let's take a look at this. Yes, I agree prayer is important to us and to God. For that is how we talk to God. More importantly, that is how He talks to us. But can we provoke the favor of God?

Is it a matter of perspective or fact? We know that grace is the unmerited favor of God, as defined by the dictionary. We also know that unmerited means something that is not earned or deserved. Clearly, we cannot earn the grace of God but we are able to provoke His attention to us. I would venture to offer that having God's attention is the epitome of favor.

God is provoked and encouraged to look in our direction when He hears our prayers and praise. He will stop what He is doing to listen. Even the angels were perplexed, "What is man that you are mindful of him the son of man that you care for him?" Ps. 8:4-5 NIV When we get the ear of God, He whispers direction; words of wisdom and knowledge. He opens up to us a universe that cannot otherwise be accessed.

Take Joseph for example. The scripture lets us in on a secret. Joseph had the favor of God and man. Joseph was the youngest child of his father's old age, at the time (prior to his brother Benjamin being born after certain events took place). He was loved so much by his father that he was given a coat of many colors. When we look at this story, do we see a spoiled, protected, young, naïve, boastful, young lad? Or are we looking at a young man who is just that, young and inexperienced? Yes, Joseph was spoiled and protected by his father. Yes, Joseph was young and naïve. He was also rotten and arrogant. Yes, he was boastful. He was the apple of his father's eye, as his father was old when Joseph was born. His brothers hated him and plotted to get rid of him. They saw the coat of many colors that their father provided to Joseph. They saw the favor that the father had for Joseph. They had no clue, however, of the favor Joseph evoked from God. Did we just determine that Joseph had the favor of God??? This certainly does not sound like favor when you discover his brother's desire to first kill him and then they sold him into slavery.

This is favor.

But let's continue. Joseph's brothers put him in a pit and sold him into slavery. They then told their father he was dead. The brothers thought they had gotten rid of their pesky younger brother with the coat of many colors. Little did they know that they were playing into the hands of God. For God was protecting Joseph the whole time. He was preparing him for the journey of a lifetime. He was preparing him to be a savior for God's people including the same brothers that wanted to see him dead. The story of Joseph is found in Genesis the 39th chapter.

The words, " The Lord was with Joseph and he prospered, and he lived in the house of his Egyptian master. When his master saw that the Lord was with him, and that the Lord gave him success in everything he did, Joseph found favor in his eyes…"

Why are we looking at Joseph's life. Joseph was righteous in God's eyesight. Joseph worshipped God. Jehovah. He did not ask to be sold into slavery. Remember, it was his father's special treatment of him and Joseph's own boasting that his brothers would one day bow down to him that made they want to get rid of him. So here we are.

What does this story have to do with the prayers of the righteous. What does grace and favor have to do with prayers of the righteous, you say. No doubt Joseph prayed to the God of Abraham, Isaac and Jacob while he was in the pit; the only God He knew. The only God he trusted. No doubt, he thought he would be killed. The scripture says there was no water in the pit. Were they expecting water to be in the pit? Rueben, one of Joseph's brothers, was planning to return to take his brother out of the pit and return him to his father, unharmed. He would not leave him there to die. But God had a change of plan.

Does not this fact strike you as odd. Maybe the brothers were hoping there would be water in the pit so they could have dropped their brother in and he would have drowned. But God had other plans. Surely this is favor and grace at work.

Did Joseph pray a particular prayer. We do not know. The scripture does not say. But let's look at the reality of the situation. The natural response to being placed in a pit to either be left to die or be sold into slavery, would put one in a state of prayer for deliverance or protection. I am sure Joseph utter a sincere petition before the Lord. Remember, it was the brother's first thought that he be killed. However, God was already at work. Rueben spoke up and said, do not kill him for it would kill our father. Even the brothers did not want the wrath of God to fall upon them for dishonoring their father in that manner. No doubt they felt that it was alright to sell him alive.

Joseph was sold into slavery. But was it slavery as we understand slavery. Yes, he had a master. Yes he was obligated to perform whatever services his master wanted. But the point to remember is, Joseph had the favor of God on him and around him. Even in his master's house he received honor. Truly the Lord looked on Joseph and touched him with grace. So that everything his hand touched blossomed. So, was it Joseph's prayer or just God's unmerited favor that was in action here? God wants to show us that he can and will do the same for us. He will provide such favor to cover us; to follow us and overtake us.

Arguably, there is a type of prayer that transforms promises to favour. Yes, I have just argued that we cannot do anything to obtain God's favor. God blesses whom He will. Let's look at some examples: Remember some of your high school friends on the softball, football or tract team. Remember how you were the best that the school had at that time. Fast forward, ten or fifteen years, you read about your fellow classmate who is now an Olympic gold medalist. Favor> Not anymore skilled than you, just favor and timing. You say to yourself, where did I go wrong. What happened? Why didn't I have the opportunity. It was not about any of that, it was clearly, the favor of God.

We cannot put ourselves in a particular position to receive favor. Yes, there are times when we need to be in the right place at the right time. But isn't that also God's will? His desire? His appointed purpose? But let's look at the record. It does not matter how pretty, beautiful, or intelligent one is. If it is not the appointed time for your success, I encourage you to wait on the Lord. Keep learning. Keep reading. Stay focused and allow the Lord to complete the work he started in you.

Can we pray and change God's mind? Look at King Hezekiah. When Hezekiah received the message that he was going to die and to get his house in order, the scripture says, he turned his face to the wall and began to entreat the Lord based on his 'works'. We know that God's favor is not released based on works. We also know that God's favor is not a product of how many prayers we send up, or how much work (good deeds) we do. So, why did God change his mind? Why did God add fifteen years to Hezekiah's life? I believe it was God exercising his prerogative to keep His promises as found throughout scripture. I also believe that God was giving us a lesson on how he can, or rather, is willing and capable of blessing. For remember, God is omnipotent, omniscient, and omnipresent. He is never lacking, always knowing, and always present.

Let's look at the number 15 in scripture. King Hezekiah enjoyed an additional fifteen years of life. Fifteen in scripture means, rest, restoration, healing and deliverance. If you look closely, you will see that all of the above life properties were exhibited in Hezekiah's blessing of extended life. Surely, King Hezekiah put forth a prevailing prayer. I believe King Hezekiah's act of 'reminding' God of the good works he had performed was the King's way of invoking God's promises, as found in Deuteronomy, chapter 28. Surely, this is an example of a faithful and unfettered prayer of a righteous man that not only availed but availed much.

What Is Prevailing Prayer

There is no doubt that Hezekiah's prayer was earnest and from his heart. Of course, he was upset that he would be dying but because of the way he lived, he could usher in an earnest prayer to be granted time to get his house in order. When it really boils down to the facts, all of us are given an opportunity to get our house in order but do we?

We do not always acknowledge or recognize that that is what God is doing when we hear the Word of the Lord preached, taught or just read or when we, ourselves, are reading the scriptures and a word of knowledge or revelation comes forth. It is God giving us another opportunity to get our house in order. But it will take prevailing prayer for Him to move us out of those tight, sometimes un-right situations.

What is an earnest, heartfelt prayer? The Amplified Bible describes it as ... The earnest (heartfelt, continued) prayer of a righteous man makes tremendous power available (dynamic in its working) James 5:16 King Hezekiah was sick unto death and God sent prophet Isaiah to inform him that he would surely die. Hezekiah's prayer in Isaiah chapter 38 invoked God's promise to overtake Him and He added 15 years to his life. The scripture says, Hezekiah, after hearing the edict from the Prophet Isaiah, that he was 'going to die and not live'; turned his face to the wall and prayed. As a result of Hezekiah's expression of his 'good works', he reminds the Lord of how he walked before the Lord in truth and with a perfect heart. Again, I refer you to Deuteronomy chapter 28:1-2. The Lord heard his prayer, saw his tears, and healed him. Hezekiah did not know it, but he invoked the promises of God. You see, healing was a promise. Rest was a promise. But an additional restorative life was favor.

To receive the full experience of the results of prayer, more particularly, earnest prayer, requires belief in God. Jesus told the Father of a demonic child, when he requested deliverance for his son, '...if thou can believe, all things are possible to him that believeth?" St. Mark 9:23. Without faith it is impossible to please God. Without faith, prayer does not work. Every door has its own key. Faith is the key to God's door. In particular, faith in Jesus, the Christ. The Son of the living God.

In Luke 8:43-48. The woman with the issue of blood experienced the healing of God because of her faith. Isn't it amazing, that with the throng of people around him, Jesus knew exactly who touched him. So doesn't it make sense that if we call him; if we entreat the throne of grace, if we seek after Him with all of our heart, energy, strength and desire, He will respond.

Let's look at Job's story. Job was singled out by God to be tested by Satan. In the Book of Job, Chapter 1 beginning verse 6, we are privy to a gathering of the sons of God coming together. The scripture says, "and Satan came also among them". God asked Satan 'why are you here? Satan answered, "From going to and fro in the earth, and from walking up and down in it." Satan was looking for someone, anyone he could abuse, misuse and cause havoc. He is still holding down that same job today.

God recommended Job. Satan knew he could not have any impact on Job's life without permission. He knew that the Lord had Job covered under His protection. He also knew that it would take God's release to attack Job. Satan was limited as to what he could do to Job. Satan is also limited as to what He can do to us. We just have to know and accept that as fact.

Job was considered by God to be a perfect and upright man. This is a story of care, comfort, promise and redemption. Satan tried everything he was allowed to try to discourage Job. All of Job's children were killed by what we now call a hurricane or tornado. All of his cattle was stolen or burned up by a fire from heaven. His camels were carried about by the Chaldeans and the servants were slain by the sword. All of these loses were committed in one day.

How did Job react. Can anyone withstand this type of loss without grumbling; without complaint; without remorse against God or someone else? Is it? Can you? Can I?

Job did. He never complained about what he was going through. In fact, Job's wife told him to just curse God and die. Was that because she did not want to see him in pain or was it a sign of her unbelief? Whatever it was, the point is about how Job handled the challenge he had been handed.

Job's patience was on display even when he was stricken with boils by Satan, as if losing his family and all of his cattle, homes, and employees was not enough, his body was attacked physically. The scripture lets us know that he was afflicted with boils from the sole of his foot unto his crown (head). How painful that must have been. Can you imagine not being able to sit, lay down, get up without pain. I would image, even trying to be still was a challenge.

Job came to an understanding and realization in his mind that no matter what the Lord allowed, he would not curse God. He knew that his hope was in God. Despite his present circumstances. Despite what his body was going through. Despite his feelings of loss for his family, his possessions; he trusted whatever the Lord had in store for him.

This is what Job came to grips with. No matter what condition he found himself, he would not curse God. He was settled in his relationship with God. He knew in whom he believed. In his own way, he gave praise to the Lord, his God. The God of Abraham, Isaac and Jacob. It is important to recognize here that there is power in praise and thanksgiving to God. Praise is a powerful tool in getting God's attention. "But thou art holy, thou that inhabits the praises of Israel." Ps. 22:3 KJV God is not bound by much. He is surely bound to show up when we praise Him and thank Him. For you see, we were created to give God glory. He loves to hear His name. I believe God will stop what He is doing when He hears true praise.

A person of praise will steer clear of murmuring. When you murmur, you limit God and favour will be far from you. "And when the people complained, it displeased the Lord and the Lord heard it and his anger was kindled, and the fire of the Lord burnt among them, and consumed them that were in the uttermost parts of the camp." Num. 11:1

Paul and Silas experienced the favour of God in prison. In the process of praising God, the prison doors were opened and their shackles fell off. All because God heard them praising and singing songs unto Him even though they were bound and in jail. I dare you to ask yourself, 'was I as faithful with my praise during a time or times when I I felt I was imprisoned? Was I faithful to the Lord and to my duties even though I did not 'feel' like going? For it is not in how we feel in the natural. The Spirit is willing but it is always the flesh that is weak. I refer you to St. Matthew chapter 26, verse 41.

When the Spirit of the Lord moves, we need to be ready. Since we know that our flesh is weak, we must learn how to depend on the Spirit of the Lord to help us move forward. We need to learn to move forward when it is not fashionable to move forward. When we have a headache, a toe ache, or a "I just want to stay home ache". It is through these small situations that we learn how to survive the bigger ones.

Paul gives us a glimpse of the hope that was held by Abraham. Abraham was 100 years of age and Sarah, his wife, was 90 at the time of their visitation by the angel of God. Gen. 18:11 KJV. They could not, by all natural standards, produce or conceive, respectively. Yet, the Lord sent an angel to tell them they would be the parents of a child in their really, really, ripe old age. Sarah laughed. I am sure Abraham was skeptic, as well. However, the scriptures do not let us in on anything that Abraham might have said or was thinking. All we know is that

Abraham moved forward with the hope that was placed in him. The Apostle Paul put it this way, "And being not weak in faith, he considered not his own body now dead, when he was about an hundred years old, neither yet the deadness of Sarah's womb:" (Rom. 4:19)

I ask myself. Did I continue to give God glory even though I was not feeling like giving Him glory? Did I have doubts about His promises to me? How can the Lord free us when we consume ourselves with murmurings and grumblings. The Psalmist said, "Enter into His gates with thanksgiving and into His courts with praise: be thankful unto Him and bless His name." Psa. 100:4 KJV

Prayer and praise will renew our mind. Prayer without praise is like bacon without eggs—a half breakfast. It will renew our strength. It will bring us before the throne room of Heaven. Without prayer it is impossible to walk in God's authority. Without praise, it is impossible to please God. We are so accustomed to reacting to circumstances, instead of learning how to respond. Prayer produces a response pleasing to God's ear. Prayer is an action that produces a reaction to events and situations that require the hand of Jesus.

What About Prayer As Confession

Prayer is a confession to the Lord of what is on your mind. Your mouth is a weapon of authority ordained by God to keep you in perfect dominion. If you say positive things based on the word of God in your heart, you will get positive results. Favor moves in the direction of those that say favorable things. "Death and life are in the power of the tongue and they that love it shall eat the fruit thereof". Prov. 18:21 KJV

If you tell me that the prayers of the righteous are not effective, I will tell you that you have never been serious about prayer. Too often, we try to calm the storm. The storm does not have to obey us. The storm obeys its maker. We need to calm ourselves. The storm will pass. Let's look at the disciples who panicked when they were caught in a storm while Jesus was sleeping in the boat.

The Apostle Mark gives us a glimpse into the minds of the disciples as they were crossing the waters while Jesus slept in the boat following what was a rather hectic several days of preaching to the multitudes of people.

"And there arose a great storm of wind, and the waves beat into the ship, so that it was now full. And He was in the hinder part of the ship, asleep on a pillow: and they awake Him, and say unto Him, Master, carest Thou not that we perish? And He arose, and rebuked the wind, and said unto the sea, Peace, be still. (The Greek word at that time meant, silence, hush). And the wind ceased, and there was a great calm. Look at St. Mark 4: 35-40 KJV-

Scripture says they were afraid. All the time they had the peace maker with them. Yet, they were afraid. The storm calmer in their presence. Jesus has authority over the storms. As long as we are in Him and He is in us, we are protected.

The scripture is clear that when they saw the winds and the waves coming into the ship they panicked. They awoke him from his sleep. These same disciples that Jesus taught, that he slept with, that he ate with, were now accusing Him of not caring. Wow! Imagine that. This man, Jesus, told them where to get money so they did not have to sleep outside, that hunger pangs would not overtake them, who taught them everything they knew even about fishing. And, they accused him of not caring. Yes, I just repeated myself. I found this to be just unbelievable. Jesus rebuked them, saying "How is it that ye have no faith?"

Was there not one of them that would stand up and acknowledge the teaching they had received from Jesus? It is time to stop letting people who do so little for us control so much of our mind, feelings and emotions. It keeps us from seeing our real friends and mentors. This is exactly what we do. We listen to everyone else but God. No doubt the disciples were listening to each other in their limited capacities. We pray but without sufficient faith to believe in the same prayers that we have just uttered.

Is there no wonder why Jesus had to rebuke them. He had to bring them back to reality.

We get so caught up in 'feeling' something that we miss the move of God. God said, He is not in the wind. He is in the still small voice. We must be calm and quiet to hear His voice. Satan brings the noise of life to get us off course. To take our focus off what we are supposed to be looking at. Prayer requires us to be quiet to hear what God has to say. Just because we do not feel excited or joyful, does not mean He is not with us.

We cannot control what happens, we can only control our reaction to events and circumstances. We must learn to become aware of our thoughts and feelings. We become unsettled because we know we are meant to do more. We have the ability to choose how we respond to outside stimuli. When we allow others to control our thoughts and actions, we lose the opportunity to be led by the Holy Spirit. Remember, the Holy Spirit does not sleep. Jesus, who sits at the right hand of His Father, never sleeps nor slumbers. He is always on His job interceding on our behalf.

Stop getting upset because someone does not agree with your thinking or someone just does not seem to get along with you. Stop trying to fit in. Remember, prayer is the key. They key to hearing. The key to listening. The key to being. Don't be afraid of being in the minority. Jesus was in the minority. Jesus was an eagle. He flew above the pigeons. Eagles fly alone. Pigeons flock together. Strive to be an eagle.

Stay calm in the face of adversity and noise. Hear the still small voice that will come. It will require you to stay calm to hear it. After hearing the still small voice, comes peace. Comes wisdom. Comes power.

Jesus spoke to the wind and said, "Peace be still."

CHAPTER 15

REFRESH AND RESTORE

God's Time For Refreshing And Restoration
Is Not Limited To Bible Days

Do you feel lost? Left out in the cold? Do you, sometimes, feel that you just do not understand what you are searching for? What is God saying? What am I supposed to be doing? What is my purpose? I was so far ahead. How did I get so far behind?

Be still. Great things are coming. When everything seems to be going wrong, just know everything, every event has a time and a season. The Book of Ecclesiastes, chapter three beginning with verse one, written by the wisest man in the Bible, and I would venture to say, the world, King Solomon, gives us a peek into this nugget of gold.

In order for the Lord to refresh and restore us, the old wine must be poured out, the vessel cleaned and sanctified before the new wine can be poured into it. This action requires patience on our part. We wait in line for hours to catch a bargain on Black Friday and Christmas Eve, even at the grocery store but we do not want to wait on God to complete the work He has started in us from the beginning. King Solomon, offers this observation, *" A man's gift maketh room for him and bringeth him before great men"* Prov. 18:16. KJV There are three areas your gift can get the attention of God. Let's take a peek, shall we?

a. <u>Prophet's Offering</u> - The widow of Zarephath and the Shunamite woman enjoyed divine favour by reason of what they gave to the prophet. (1 Kgs. 17:10-24 and 2 Kgs. 4:1-37). What is this prophet's reward? The prophet's reward is the fulfillment of the prophetic word. While I am sure that there are other ways to obtain a prophet's reward, I can only think of two right now.

   1. Do what the prophet does. Trust and obey.
   2. To receive a prophet as a prophet. This means even though you may not have heard the word from God for yourself, you trust and obey the word of the prophet to the point that you act on it by faith.

God speaks to His prophets all day. All night. He does not give any one prophet all of his direction. He reserves the right to share His revelation between several for protection and deliverance as needed. In other words, the enemy will not be able to steal, kill or destroy the work of redemption because of Christ.

Neither can the enemy steal, kill or destroy your purpose when God distributes his word through many different prophets even at different times. Remember, the word says out of the mouth of two or three witnesses let all things be established.

b. <u>Giving to the Poor</u> – When you give to the needy, through a heart of love, you provoke God's interest. "He that hath pity upon the poor lendeth unto the Lord; and that which he hath given will he pay him again." Prov. 19:17

   Jesus reminded us when He spoke to the multitude and gave the Sermon on the Mount, that when we feed our spiritual poverty, happiness comes to us. The Prophet Malachi said, give and it will be given back to you, pressed down, shaken together and running over.

Remember, all of us have needs. Being poor is more than having a lack of money. It can be lack of spirit; lack of joy; lack of companionship. Be more willing to give. Do it without grudging. Give with a smile. Without looking for a return. Remember, giving does not necessarily mean money. It can be services. A listening ear. A card. A smile. A compliment.

c. <u>Giving to your Parents</u> - "Honour thy father and mother, (which is the first commandment with promise) that it may be well with thee, and thou mayest live long on the earth." Eph. 6:2-3

Honoring your parents is commanded by God all through scripture. From the Old Testament, in the book of Leviticus to the New Testament, in the book of Ephesians. The writer of the book of Leviticus helps us to understand that honoring our parents is compared to honoring God. Specifically, every person must respect his/her mother and father.

Your gift to your parents irrespective of their wealth or wickedness will provoke the promises of God. God is a lover of parents. He honored his parents. He wants us to honor ours. Jesus provided care for his mother while He was hanging on the cross. In fact, He gave charge of his mother to John, the Beloved.

Paul, the Apostle, wrote in his epistle to the Ephesians, that if we as children want to be wise, we must listen to our parents and do what they tell us, and the Lord will help us. The first commandment with promise was "Honor your father and mother". The promise that was/is attached is that you will prosper and live a long, full life.

I challenge you to try any or all of these steps. I promise, you will not be disappointed.

Giving in General

Learning to give is a true gift. The gift of giving is a gift of love. Learn to love without condition. Talk without bad intentions. Give without bad reason and most of all, care for people without expectation.

It is important, no it is imperative that we live such a life to be able to cross the threshold into new dimensions of love; new dimensions of peace; new dimensions of joy; new dimensions of wisdom and understanding. New dimensions in Christ.

We must show respect to people who have not earned it, not as a reflection of their character, but as a reflection of our Christ in us. This is a pinnacle state. It was not until Saul became arrested and converted by the power of God that he understood the power of giving. I employ you to read his story in the Book of Acts, Chapter 9. It will not matter what version of the Bible you read it in, just read it.

It will change your life. Then you will understand, the press that Apostle Paul spoke about in Phillipians 3:14.

CHAPTER 16

BE KINGDOM FOCUSED

It is important for us to seek first the kingdom of God and his righteousness and then all these things shall be added.
– St. Matt. 6:33

What things? All of the pleasures of life. Good health, prosperity of mind, heart and finances.

Let's not get ahead of ourselves. First, let's explore what or who the kingdom of God is. Keep in mind, the razor blade is sharp but cannot cut a tree; the axe is strong but cannot cut a hair. Anything called a kingdom is a place where someone called a king has dominion. What is dominion? Dominion is having sovereignty or total control.

No king or queen can have dominion unless he/she can claim ownership over territory. Take Queen Elizabeth II, for example. She is the reigning monarch of the United Kingdom and other commonwealth realms. A realm is a kingdom. Queen Elizabeth II has control over the territories that make up the United Kingdom and its commonwealth. If you study kingdoms and how they function, you learn that everything becomes subject to the king's authority. Everything, every office, every governmental department must get permission from the Queen to function. This includes all churches, hospitals, libraries, museums and businesses including private (sole ownership as we call them) businesses. Everyone in the King or Queen's domain must give precedence and honor to His or Her Majesty. As long as the Queen's subjects obey the laws and regulations that have been provided under her authority, they will receive the benefits as loyal citizens or subjects.

The President of the United States does not have dominion, nor does he own the whole country. The prime minister of England does not own the country he governs, and neither does the Queen. But in a true kingdom, everything becomes part of the king's personal property. The psalmist tells us that the cattle on a thousand hills and the hills belong to God. Psalm 50, a psalm of Asaph. It is a reminder that God claims the world as His. That everything and everyone belongs to Him! For He is the one that pushed back the oceans to permit dry ground to appear. He planted firm foundations. He created trees and flowers to grow continually by implanting within them their own specific seed. Does this thought help to challenge you to re-read Psalm 50 with an open mindset?.

If we are to seek the greater of God, then we must prepare ourselves. We cannot go into His kingdom without being properly prepared spiritual, naturally, emotionally and physically. God has rules that must be met. Like with any other monarch, there is a protocol that must be adhered to. Even the children of Israel were required to wash themselves, sanctify themselves including not 'going into their wives' for three days before they could approach the Mountain to hear the voice of the Lord. We must be committed to whatever it takes if we want to enjoy the greater of God.

God, YHWH (Yahweh in English) as the Hebrews called Him. The God of Abraham, Isaac and Jacob; the creator of mankind is the true King. We cannot understand the kingdom of God unless we study it. We must see it modeled. How can we know about the kingdom of God if it is not taught. Who can teach the kingdom except those who have studied and understand kingdom principles.

God is the supreme ruler and monarch of the heavens and the earth. He and Jesus, his Son who sits on His right hand, govern the spiritual powers. If we seek the kingdom of God and His righteousness, we then seek to be where He is. Where He has domain. If we honor Him and his rules then we shall have good success. Do not complain. When you complain you make yourself a victim. Be the victor. Rejoice in the freedom that is Christ.

If we are faithful to Him and His commands, as set forth in the Holy Bible, we shall reap the good of the land. Jesus told us, "And if I go to prepare a place for you, I will come again, and receive you unto myself; that where I am, there ye may be also. St. John 14:3 KJV

God has given each of us our own uniqueness and our own purpose. Do not covet someone else's gift(s). Because the Lord has gifted you in a particular area, do not look down on anyone unless you are admiring their footwear. Yes, we are still talking about reaching thresholds into greater glory. Let's be clear, however, there is no one, two, or three point plan to reaching God's glory. The greater glory of God is real. And, it requires sincere devotion to keeping the entire Word of the Lord. I heard that thought,. You are correct, no one on this earth is perfect. However, we can be like Paul and press toward the mark of the prize of the higher calling in Christ Jesus. We must strive, every day to live holy unto the Lord.

But seek ye first the kingdom of God and his righteousness and all these things shall be added unto you." Matt. 6:33. While there are a number of ways to seek the kingdom of God, let's talk about a few:

1. Soul winning: Matt. 28:19-20 Your practical involvement with God in His purpose for reaping the over-ripe harvest of souls guarantees His divine attention.

2. Sacrifices: Sacrificial giving towards God's kingdom or business is trigger for divine favor in second Chron. 1:6-7. Solomon offered a thousand burnt offerings and God gave him a blank check which signifies unusual favor.

3. <u>Faithfulness</u>: 1 Cor. 4:2. Prov. 28:20. Moreover, it is required in stewards that a man be found faithful." 1 Cor. 4:2 "A faithful man shall abound with blessings; but he that maketh haste to be rich shall not be innocent". Prov. 28:20. Joseph's faithfulness ensures his continuous favour. He said, "How then can I do this great wickedness and sin against God? Gen. 39:9 A faithful man, after God has blessed him, will not miss his tithes. He will not forget about his service in the House of God.

It is imperative that we remain connected to God. Hosea 12:13 "And by a prophet, the Lord brought Israel out of Egypt, and by a prophet was he preserved". Hos. 12:13. After God has blessed Joseph in a strange land, He did not forget his root. A branch that is cut off from a tree will die a natural death. When God blesses you don't forget your root.

4. <u>Live in forgiveness</u>. Gen. 45:7 "And God sent me before you to preserve you a posterity in the earth and to save your lives by a great deliverance" Gen. 45:7. Joseph despite all that his brethren did to him, even when he had opportunity to revenge, he did not". David had several opportunities to avenge the wickedness of Saul against him but he refused. No wonder David also enjoyed continuous favour from God.

5. <u>Live in obedience</u>. Gen. 2:22 – Abraham enjoyed constant favor from God because he lived a life of total obedience. Even after God has blessed him with a child after waiting many years, he obeyed God and offered the child for sacrifice. Saul lost the throne despite God's promise to his generation to sit on the throne forever due to disobedience.

6. <u>Be joyful</u>. Isaiah 12:3 – Joseph did not complain for one day even despite the experiences he went through. He was so charming even as a slave that the madam of the house wanted to sleep with him.

Even in prison, because he was full of joy he was made the head of other prisoners. One way to enjoy constant favor from God is to always display joy irrespective of what you are passing through. "Therefore with joy shall ye draw water out of the wells of salvation." Isa. 12:3

7. Live a life of thanksgiving. "Let us come before his presence with thanksgiving and make a joyful noise unto him with Psalms" Ps. 95:2. "Be careful for nothing, but in everything by prayer and supplication with thanksgiving let your request be made known unto God". Philip 4:6. Brethren, it takes thanksgiving to provoke favor of God and it also takes thanksgiving to enjoy continuous favor. An adage says, "When a child thanks an elder for yesterday's blessing, he will definitely get another one. Most Israelites died in the wilderness because they forgot the God that delivered them from Egypt and began to complain." And when the people complained, it displeased the Lord; and the Lord heard it and his anger was kindled; and the fire of the Lord burnt among them and consumed them that were in the uttermost parts of the camp. Num. 11:1 KJV Fellow believers, continuous favour from God requires a life of daily thanksgiving. A person of thanksgiving will not have any cause to complain or grumble. Anyone that complains will never experience God's blessings.

Let me explain this a bit further. If we are honest with ourselves, we will all have some periods, some experiences that we "share" with someone, in the physical realm, to help us get through the pressures of life. Some people do not call this sharing complaining. Some people do. Having said this, I would like to give a personal definition as to what I believe constitutes complaining. I believe that the Lord is saying anything that encompasses the same event, the same circumstance(s); that he has to constantly, every day, every phone call, every encounter; every prayer, hear over and over again, constitutes a complaint. When the Word tells us that we are to give our griefs and burdens to Him (the

Lord), we are also supposed to and expected to leave them with Him. Not take them back. For what good is all the lamenting if we only bring back the same trouble that we went to leave? We are to forget those things which are behind. Be a tomorrow thinker.

Now that we have established what constitutes complaining. Let's move forward to a better understanding as to why this upsets the Lord. Complaining removes us from faith. And faith is the means by which we move forward to and in God. Faith is our means of transportation to Jesus. As the Apostle Paul encouraged the saints in the Book of Hebrews, chapter 11, verse 6, "But without faith it is impossible to please him (God): for he that cometh to God must believe that he is, and that he is a rewarder of them that diligently seek him. KJV

Without belief in Jesus, the Son of God, there is no greater glory. There is no hope of salvation.

CHAPTER 17

RESIST THE ENEMY

Submit yourselves therefore to God. Resist the devil and he will flee from you.
– James 4:7 KJV

As saints, agents, ministers, ambassadors of Christ, we weep and cry out to the Lord for a message of comfort and hope for all. People are hurting in a myriad of ways. We pray for addicts, alcoholics, the homeless, the lost, the forgotten. We pray for those that are downtrodden, those who have been left to die. Those who have lost hope in Christ and themselves.

King Solomon give us kingdom revelations and powerful words to live by. While I have always found the Books of Proverbs and Ecclesiastes interesting and informative, I have learned that it is also kingdom teachings. Proverbs 16:18 allows us this insight, "Pride goeth before destruction, and a haughty spirit before a fall." The best method or ammunition to defeat the enemy is to use humility.

Boasting does not guarantee success. Boasting, in fact, becomes a prophecy of a future failure. Unless we are boasting in the Lord, the God and Creator of heaven and earth, then failure is imminent. Without God's strength. Without His power. There is no future. We have no strength of our own.

God gives grace to the humble, as the Apostle James reminds us in verse 6 of chapter 4 of his missive. In order to resist the enemy, the devil, it is imperative that we learn how to be humble.

Sometimes our prayer goes something like this:

> Father, it seems that everywhere we turn, we see pain and sorrow. Grief and despair. What message, Lord can I bring to those who are in such need? What word can I give someone? How can I help without appearing boastful? For it is not my intent. I merely want to help, Lord. Give me the words to say. But more importantly, allow my life to be the example. Allow your presence to flow through me so that someone, anyone, can see that you exist and are waiting.

> Father, allow the opening of ears and hearts to receive your words of hope and peace. Let them know that you are able to heal, deliver and make whole. That we do not allow the enemy to overtake us. That you have given us the necessary ammunition to defeat our oppressor.

> Help, O'God those who lift up their eyes to you for direction, for hope, for help. Those who have expressed the desire and will to want to move forward in you. Who want to accept you, Christ, as their personal Saviour. Those, who want to live and learn about your Kingdom.

Let us look at Daniel's three friends who were subjected to being placed in the fiery furnace. King Nebuchadnezzar was full of fury after he had issued an edict that all of the citizens of Babylon were to bow down at his image.

Laying out a little history …Daniel and his three friends, Hananiah (Shadrach), Mishael (Meshach) and Azariah (Abednego) were children of Israel who were carried into the land of Babylon after Jerusalem was besieged. They were children of the Most High God. Upright and dedicated to their belief in the true and living God.

The edict that King Nebuchadnezzar sent out required its citizenry to bow at his image. They refused to worship King Nebuchadnezzar.

They only worshipped the God of Abraham, Isaac and Jacob. As a result, of their disobedience to the king, they were to be cast in a fiery furnace. For the punishment of failing to worship the king was death.

Here, Mishael, Azariah and Hananiah expressed their boldness and positivity in their true God. They boasted on God and His powers not their own. Specifically saying to King Nebuchadnezzar, "If it be so, our God, whom we serve, is able to deliver us from the burning fiery furnace, and he will deliver us out of thine hand, O king." Dan. 3:17, KJV.

We have been talking about humility. It is one thing to be boastful in ones self. It is another to be boastful in God! Truly, the Hebrew boys had humbled themselves before God to allow His presence and His power to take precedent. They knew within themselves, they had no power. But their God did and still does.

As a result of their humility and their faith to allow God to act, they entered the furnace. Bound in their coats, their stockings, their turbans and their other garments, they were cast into the midst of the burning fiery furnace. The order went out that the furnace was to be heated seven times hotter than it was usually heated. When Nebuchadnezzar order this, he did not realize that he was playing into the hand of the true and living God.

One of the meanings of the number seven in scripture is God's perfection and completeness. E.W. Bullinger, Numbers in Scripture, Kregel Publications 1986 When I look at this term, I think about the fact that God was tired of King Nebuchadnezzar harassing his children. I believe this was a sign to the three believers that He, God was ready to make his move on their behalf and show these people, this king, who He (God) really is.

The furnace was so hot that even those who were charged with heating it died from the heat on the outside of the furnace.

I believe these three brave children had all of the clothes they came with on their backs. It was the effort of the soldiers to make sure they burned without recognition to set an example for others who would defy the king's edict.

These three young men fell down, bound, in the fiery furnace. Sometimes life hands us a fiery furnace. It appears that everything is breaking down; that no one cares. That we have on every stitch of clothing we can carry just so the flames would engulf us quickly. But God, who sits high and looks low, casts in His own time, a cool breeze; a protection from the heat and the flame because of our faith in Him. He places a flame retardant over us to keep us from burning up under the assault of the enemy.

We must remember that is because of their humility. Because they were willing to give up their choice to follow the choices the Lord had in store for them. It was because they reduced themselves in the sight of God that He could deliver them in His might.

Even King Nebuchadnezzar was astounded when he looked into the furnace and saw four men in the furnace. He said, "Did we not cast three men bound into the midst of the fire? The King then said, but I see four men loose, walking in the midst of the fire, and they have no hurt; and the form of the fourth is like the son of God." Daniel 3:25 KJV

God has a peculiar way of working things out for us. When we brag on Him. When we permit faith to be embraced instead of fear. When we resist the devil, we invite the greater glory of God in our midst.

CHAPTER 18

HUMILITY

Jesus said, "If anyone desires to come after Me, let him deny himself, and take up his cross and follow Me."

– St. Luke 9:23, NKJV

If anyone desires. This is a strong statement. I looked up the word "desire". To desire means to have a strong feeling of wanting to have something or wishing for something to happen. Paul, the Apostle, encouraged the saints in his second letter to the Corinthians, "For if there is first a willing mind, it is accepted and according to what one has, and not according to what he does not have. " (2 Cor. 8:12 KJ) If there is no willing mind to come to Christ, then the coming is of no value. For Jesus said, we must deny ourselves. In other words, we must deny our flesh. We cannot take up our cross and carry the flesh at the same time.

There must first be a willing mind. This opens our eyes to show us the meaning of humility or modesty in relation to others and how we treat them. I had a conversation with a County official in my home area, about some land that we were looking at for the church. The issue before us was irrigation. In other words the land must be low enough to allow proper water runoff to avoid flooding. The Spirit of the Lord stopped me in my tracks. I heard God say, ' I cannot make your life fruitful if you are not low enough to avoid becoming high minded. ' It was all I could do to hold back the tears.

During the meeting, I shared the vision for the ministry God had given me. Specifically, to offer Christ as Lord and Saviour to those who are seeking refuge and love; to house the elderly and senior pastors who have been forgotten or were at the mercy of a church that was unable to help care for their faithful shepherds and widows, in deed. Those who had served for twenty years or more without remuneration. We are sent to provide instruction to the young and older alike. Instruction in the Word of God and in the natural world. We are sent to provide wisdom, knowledge and practical teaching, as well as spiritual teaching to the young and the more mature in age. We are sent to provide clothes and food to those who are in need.

I remembered being so hurt that I was unable to provide for a single mother with three children that I had promised and for whom I had set aside food . I went to work that morning and expected to return to the church after work to pick up food for this particular family only to find that someone had stolen everything we had. Seriously, if there were any bugs around even they would have left us an angry note. All I could do was sit on the steps and cry. How could I help this family. We had nothing. I, personally, did not have enough money to go to the store and buy more food. At that moment, I felt alone and defeated. I was broken. My heart hurt so much. My emotions were running wild. I went from being hurt, to being defeated, to be being betrayed.

My tears and my hurt turned into questioning. Why would you allow us to do this work for so long only to Iet us down now when this family of children are dependent upon receiving this food. I could not curse God because I know deep on the inside that He must have a plan. But that did not stop the hurt.

I began to remind the Lord of what He already knew. Why do we do this. Why do we feel the need to remind God. He does not forget anything but our sins. Yet, in my humanness, I continued to press, 'we are only trying to help those who are in need. You know that we love the people. Why, God. Why at this particular time, when children are in need.'

I had decided, I would just buy whatever I could afford with what I had. I also said, in my mind, I would not do food ministry again. The Lord brought the word of the Psalmist back to me, "Why art thou cast down, O my soul? And why art thou disquieted in me? Hope thou in God: for I shall yet praise him for the help of his countenance." Ps. 42:5 (KJV)

I had barely gotten this verse off my lips, when the Lord sent an angel. An angel in the form of one of our newer evangelists who had come to the church to pray on her way home. When she saw me sitting on the steps crying, immediately she said, 'what happened, what can I do?". Then, another one of our saints showed up. I told her what happened. And that I did not have enough money to get enough groceries for this family. She said, Pastor, don't worry. We will work this together". Look at God. He always has a ram in the bush! If we are faithful and obedient. Wow!

We prayed together that the Lord would stretch what we had for the benefit of this needy family. We proceeded together to the grocery store. Thanking God for His Word of faith in action and in advance for favor to obtain everything that was needed. The Lord moved so through our words of compassion that as we spoke with the manager of the store, he gave us additional foods to help in this situation. Only God can do this. I will admit, I had said, I would not provide food service again. I was just through. I felt that my heart had been torn out of my chest. But, God is the judge and the healer of hurts and broken hearts. I did not stop providing food to the needy, the homeless, and less fortunate individuals and families.

It is important to keep in mind from where God has brought us. None of us were born with silver spoons in our mouths. Even the richest of families did not get that way over night. Someone paid the price. If we forget the struggles, the hard times, we lose ourselves. And most importantly, we lose our respect for each other and for life.

God wants us to be humble. We cannot be effective for Him, if we have a haughty spirit. A spirit that is seen before the Spirit that is felt is empty. We are encouraged to show the spirit of the Lord and not our own spirit. Carrying the cross requires humility. King Solomon said, 'a haughty spirit goeth before a fall'.

> *Sometimes you have to experience what*
> *you don't want in life to come to a full*
> *understanding of what you do want.* The MindsJournal

We must remember to always give God His honor. Whatever is performed or accomplished, it is because of God. He should get the glory.

Do not try to steal God's glory. We can never reach the greater glory of God with pride going before us. I believe it is the Lord's will that we will see the legacy of hope and faith in Christ come to fruition. I believe it is God's will that we are to care for each other. Humility will bring us together. Humility, I believe is the connecting ladder to the threshold of greater glory in God.

"If the earnestness is there, the gift is acceptable. " 2 Corinthians 8:12 New International Version. We must be earnest to give to God and to others. Not with a grudging mind or slow hand. But with an open heart. The Berean Literal Bible puts it this way, *"For if the readiness is present, it is acceptable as if he might have, not as he does not have."* Be always ready to give from what you have, not looking at what you do not have. It is the giving heart that creates the bridge to freedom. The bridge to warmth. The bridge to joy. The bridge to prosperity. The bridge to humility.

Let's look at Ruth for a minute. This is a story of great humility. She was married to a believer in God, even though she originally was not a believer. Her husband died and she, her sister-in-law who were Moabite widows, along with their mother in law, Naomi, found themselves returning back to Bethlehem. Bethlehem means place of bread. This is important here because Naomi came from Bethlehem and was not, after her husband and two sons died, returned to the place of bread. A place where she could get nourishment.

Sometimes the grass looks greener on the other side of the road. Or in someone else's yard. Until you get up close on it. Then you see the same bare spaces that exists in your yard. Ruth and Naomi found themselves returning to Bethlehem where Naomi's family resided. No doubt they had been gone for many years. Ruth's humility to work in the field to obtain food for she and her mother-in-law brought her before a great man.

It is important to say here, that if we allow humility to take charge, we will be forever full. We will not lack. Humility will bring you before great men and women. Humility will open doors that money cannot open.

Seek to stay humble before the Lord and before man. Seek to encourage others above yourself. To seek the greater glory of God requires consistency of humility.

CHAPTER 19

TAKE TIME TO
RECONSIDER

"The best thing about the worst time of your life
Is that you get to see the true colors of yourself."

My grandson and I were on our way to his pre-op appointment which was four hours away from where he lives in Georgia. We stopped for breakfast at a Waffle House. I am so accustomed to being alone, I headed for the door of the restaurant, after finally extracting myself from his very low vehicle, without thought. I noticed him running up behind me. He said, "no, Grandma, I will get the door".

This is what God is saying to us. Let Him get the door. Stop moving so fast. We move in our own strength, in our own mind without waiting on Him. He wants to open the door for you. He is a gentleman. Allow him to open the door.

I had to challenge myself. I was forced to take inventory of my own actions and my own heart. Am I running too fast. Am I in such a hurry that I almost missed it? Slow down, I heard Him say. So I say to you. Slow down. Take time to hear the voice of the Lord for direction. Stop trying to rush God. Sometimes we move too fast for our own good. We live in a hurry, hurry, world. Some of you came up in the microwave generation, some are now in the one-pot generation. Whatever the generation, we try to put God in one of those categories.

The earth is the Lord's and the fullness thereof;
The world and they that dwell therein. Ps. 24:1 KJV

Since the earth was created by God, and we know it belongs to Him, He has no reason to rush His work. God pushed back the waters to allow dry ground to be visible. He placed two major objects in the sky to provide sufficient light for its purpose; namely, the sun and the moon. He provides seasons and times to allow for growth of seeds and death and sleep when necessary.

Since God created time from within Himself, since He provided us with day and night; a period of rest and period of work, why do we continue to push ourselves and His creations faster than what He has spoken? Admittedly, we all have the same twenty-four hours in a day. We all have the same amount of time to worship, grow, develop, create and serve. Why do we always seem to run out of time? Why do we push ourselves to do more to obtain natural resources and less time seeking more of a spiritual connection with God, our Creator?

We need to take time to reconsider our priorities. Take time to seek more from our relationship with the Lord, our Maker. David gave us a hint of how to seek more of God in Psalm 23, affectionally known as —the Good Shepherd psalm. The King James version, verse three, puts it this way, "He restoreth my soul: he leadeth me in the paths of righteousness for his name's sake." In the Passion Translation of the same verse, David's thoughts are expressed, as I interpret loosely, the circling of the sheep on Israel's hillside as they climb higher and higher. This climbing eventually forms a path that keeps leading them closer and closer to the Lord.

Sometimes we think we are going in circles when really, we are going higher. It takes time to climb the mountain. David led the sheep in a wide circular motion so they would be able to grip the mountain side and not become dizzy and fall off as they continued their climb. Consider that the Lord takes us up the mountain in a circular motion to reduce the challenges of falling; or becoming dizzy and losing pace. Stop rushing the process. There is a good reason we have twenty-four hours in a day. There is a good reason that God created rest time for these bodies. For these human minds. Without rest, these mortal bodies would fall apart. We would become babbling idiots.

The Greeks have two words for time. Chronos and Kairos. Chronos represents the chronological or sequential time that we use every day to set our watches, our calendars. We, as human beings run our lives on sequential time schedules. The second word, kairos, represents God's opportune moment. I encourage you to seek to be lead by kairos time. Seek to understand that God has an opportune moment for each of us. Seek to learn how to tap into God's kairos time.

We can never do more than what God requires or move faster or take more classes to get in God's good graces. He has an opportune time for all things. Ask God to examine your motives for doing what you do. Ask yourself why am I doing this? What is my purpose for acting this way? Will my actions please God or are they set to please me?

We must reconsider our ways, our thoughts. We must take heed that we do not our alms before men to be seen of them. Sometimes it is necessary for us to sit on the second row. Let someone else take the front seat. Stop coming into the church or the meeting 'fashionably late' to be seen. Come in early. Set the spiritual tone that invites God. Take time to learn to become one with the Lord. We must allow ourselves to be free to hear His voice.

Reconsider why you want Christ in your life. Why you want to be a servant for the Lord. Why you want to preach, teach the gospel of Jesus, the Christ? Do not be sidetracked by the anniversary programs, religious celebrations, the offerings. Not all receive those things. Yes, the laborer is worthy of his/her hire but not every religious or non-profit organization can financially provide their shepherd with a salary or housing allowance. Many of our churches still are not receiving enough tithes and offerings to pay musicians and deacons and others who perform needed services around the building to help keep it up let alone their leadership. Yet, there are still many who do have these means. If your local assembly does not, do not be discouraged. We must be willing to work out of our soul's salvation through love. For God is the judge and will take care of our every need.

I had the pleasure of seeing and hearing Dr. Cindy Trimm in person at a conference in Maryland. I will always remember her comment to the listeners. "**Do not let who you are today, sabotage your tomorrow.**" I have since discovered this comment was made in her book, "Hello Tomorrow!", published by Charisma House. Then I came across this thought from E-buddism.com, "*If you can't do anything about it, then let it go. Don't be a prisoner to things you cannot change.*"

These two thoughts are not mutually exclusive of one another. They are clear reminders that we are not to think of ourselves more highly than we ought, as the Apostle Paul reminded the church in Romans 12:3. We are to remember that "it is in Him we move and live and have our being"; not by anything that we can or have done or think we can do. Neither are we to dwell on those things that we do not have the power to change. Such attitudes will only hinder our growth and faith in God in whom we are to trust. Use them to help us remember to reconsider our ways and our thoughts. That our thoughts and our actions are to direct others to Christ, not us.

Stop expecting to be reimbursed, by this world's standards, for everything you do. Stop seeking the approval of man. Seek God's approval. If we seek the approval of man, we have our reward here. Is it worth it? Does man's approval out weight God's reward? Is it worth man's approval to lose out on what our Heavenly Father has for us?

God provided an overabundance of blessings for us that have been set out in the book of Deuteronomy, chapter 28. Specifically, if we hearken diligently, if we observe and do all His commands. Who is 'His'? "His" is God. If we follow these directions, all of the blessings shall come to pass. In other words, God's promises to us will manifest. In fact, these promises will overtake us.

"Seek ye first the kingdom of God and his righteousness and all of these things shall be added unto you." St. Matt. 6:33. Jesus provided this word of comfort, this promise, to the disciples and those who were hearing his teachings while he was on the Mount. He said, do not worry about where you will stay or what you will eat. If I send you, I will provide.

We must seek a stable mind in the midst of an unstable world. If all you have ever seen is poverty, if all you have ever seen is domestic violence, if all you have ever seen is betrayal, you become attracted to what you are exposed to. Even though you say you do not want it, you end up wanting what your normal is. How do I keep getting tied up with the wrong man? How is it I cannot hold a job? Because that is the only examples you have ever seen. It is your norm. In the gospel of St. John, chapter 9, verse 2, the disciples asked Jesus who sinned, he or his parents, that he was born blind? "If you were born blind, all you know is darkness.

It is not until we experience or are introduced to another way of life that we know we have a choice. Do not be like Adam and Eve who traded glory clothes for fig leaves. Instead, trade fig leaves for glory clothes. Even though we say we do not want the same life, the same experiences that we have grown up in and around. The same normal. We find ourselves wondering, " Why do I keep getting tied up with the wrong people?"

I had a conversation, recently, with an individual who has lived in the country all of her life. Let me preface this by saying, I am not against, nor am I putting down, my friend. I am merely sharing a point. There are no streetlights, no major shopping areas less than three hours away from her home. No internet accessibility. When she comes to visit here, she is always amazed at her surroundings. As long as she is at home, she does not miss or see the lack. She never realized there were so many different more comfortable surroundings. So many opportunities that have not been available to her because of where she lives. On one hand she desires to live in the city so that she may experience some of the missed opportunities. Yet, she is held back because of her mind.

Because she is afraid. She is afraid she would get lost on the subway. She is afraid to drive in the city. She is afraid of working in a big city. Why is she afraid? Because she would be outside of her comfort zone. She is not accustomed to the traffic patterns in the city. Too many cars, she says. She is not accustomed to the people. Too many people, she says. She is afraid to move forward because of her limited life exposure. Oh, yes, the money sounds good—the things she could purchase; the bills she could pay. But she is being held back by her mind. I asked her to reconsider the 'what' and the 'why' of her desires to stay and/or to leave.

Many of us are the same way. It may not be because we live in the country. We are all held back by something. Remember the story of the elephant. The elephant had been tethered by a chain around its ankle for years. He realizes he can only go ten feet away from his bonds. When the chain is removed and replaced by a rope, he still does not wander further than ten feet from where his iron bonds would have taken him. Why, because in his mind, he is still bound. He has not tried the rope to determine if it is as strong as the iron. He automatically believes that one bond is as strong as the next bond. His mind had not been changed.

We cannot reach the greater glory of God if we are bound in our minds. Everything, every action and inaction begins in the mind. Many of us are afraid to move forward for fear of things that are outside our norm. Jesus is saying, trust me. Let me help you reconsider so that you may grow in My grace. For my grace is sufficient! Let's look at a story in St. John, chapter 9 which references Jesus healing a man who was born blind. The disciples asked him, who sinned. Jesus said, no one. This sickness happened to him so that you could watch him experience God's miracle. Sometimes sickness or other events are allowed to help us grow in our faith. Help us to see the miraculous God that we serve. Jesus said, it is day and we must work the works of Him that sent us, while it is day.

Sometimes we must stop where we are and take note of our specific actions. We are constantly moving. Going here and there. We get caught up in the doing to be doing roller coaster. We become so tired of doing the same things day after day after day. We become burned out with church, burned out with work, burned out with family responsibilities. We see only the work. We have become so performance minded that we have forgotten the why for the performance.

Reconsider the why. Anytime we only look at the outward, we will always see the flesh and not the spirit. Jesus said, *"Come unto me and I will give you rest."* How can I rest when my mind is bound? I cannot change, I cannot move, I cannot reconsider so long as I am bound in my mind. In the parable of the prodigal son, found in St. Luke, chapter 15, after the rich man's son left home with everything he thought he was entitled to receive before the death of his father, he found himself left with nothing. All of his friends left when his money left. He found himself fighting to eat with the pigs in the pig's pen. Can you imagine this. The second son found himself, no longer living in a castle with all the servants and all the food and whatever types and kinds of food you could ever want, only to find yourself now, lost, stinky, broke, no friends, and fighting to eat whatever the pigs are eating? The scripture is clear that he was destitute.

Nothing had changed. He was still stinky, still worn, still shoeless, still in the same now tattered clothes, still in the pig's pen. But the scripture said, he came to himself. In order to reconsider our ways, sometimes it requires us to first become lost so that we can be found. Sometimes it requires that the Lord will allow us to get our backs up against a wall so that we have nowhere else to go.

Come to yourself. Ask the Lord to help you come to yourself before your back gets up against a wall. Before you become shoeless, coatless and hungry. Before you leave home only to wind up being embarrassed to return. I see this young man repenting in his heart. Crying in the pig pen. Lord, help me. Forgive me for being such a sorry son. So unappreciative of what you had allowed my father to provide. So unappreciative of where I was and what you had bestowed upon me. So unappreciative of the kind father that taught me and fed me and clothed me. Forgive me, Lord. Allow me to return to my father's house and seek forgiveness.

We need to ask the Lord to give us a heart of reconciliation. Sometimes we need to be reconciled unto our own self before we can be reconciled to someone else. It is important to reconsider how we think. Reconsider how we react to events. Before we respond to what someone is saying, reconsider how it sounds, how our responses will affect others. Remember, it is what comes out of the mouth that destroys. So let us reconsider our ways so that we sin not against each other or against God, our Father.

As the Lord moves to prosper us monetarily, we should not forget the why that started it. King Solomon wrote in the Book, Ecclesiastes chapter 10 verse 19, "A feast is made for laughter, and wine maketh merry: but money answereth all things." KJV In Paul's epistle to Pastor Timothy, he wrote 'For the love of money is the root of all kinds of evil, which while some coveted after, they have erred from the faith, and pierced themselves through with may sorrows. 1 Tim. 6:10 (New Scofield Reference Bible). This is not a contradiction. King Solomon was addressing the times in which he lived. The foolishness of kings to throw parties for the love of it. The fact that they had all the money they needed to bring them the limited joy they graved. Or was it really, joy? Paul was teaching the new Pastor Timothy, that it is okay to enjoy money. It is okay to have money. The problem comes from loving money more than loving God.

Any persons in business or wanting to do business knows it costs money to hire individuals to tape, record, publish and market. Business costs. No matter what type of business it is. Do not begrudge anyone who is able to have reached a particular status to become a business owner or to have climbed the ranks in another man's business to be able to afford certain pleasures of life.

Do be cognizant of the purpose for which you are doing what you do. Are you meeting the need that you were called to meet? Or did you get sidetracked by pride and ego? In our efforts to reach others to deliver the gospel, did we forget about those who have minimal resources? Did we lose sight on the real meaning of what we were called to do? Let us reconsider the why.

All of us from time to time are industrious. Otherwise why work. Why seek to be promoted if not for more money. At some point it is not about meeting just our needs but we should be helping to meet the needs of some who are less fortunate. I am not talking about individuals who have deliberately deprived themselves. I am talking about those who have been working, either in the home or outside; those whose lives have been stricken by some indeliberate act or action beyond their control and need a helping hand. I believe we are to seek to help the poor and the needy, but not the greedy. Jesus teaches us to do good. To help those who are less fortunate.

It is important to note that money in and of itself does not answer everything. It will neither feed nor clothe; but it is an instrument of commerce. It does address the necessities of life. Necessities such as rent or mortgage payments, groceries. Yes, it answers clothing requirements. So, why did the great wise King Solomon make the statement, 'money answereth all things'? I believe King Solomon was addressing our nature life. It does not answer anything of the soul. It cannot pay for the pardon of sin. Nor the favor of God or the peace of conscience.

Even as I write this missive, even as I pray it touches many lives and helps to change many circumstances for the better, I pray with each word, each chapter, that I do not forget my purpose. We must keep our God-given purpose always in the front of our minds.

I encourage you to stay focused on the Word of the Lord. Be faithful and committed to your local pastors and leaders who have proven their commitment to you and to Jesus the Christ. Stay focused on loving one another as Christ has loved us. Humility is always in fashion.

We must reconsider how we receive the Word of the Lord. Never put one another down because one does not sound like, or act like another. There are many members but one body. When we walk around with a negative attitude we affect everyone around us. If we criticize everyone and everything that is said, we bring infection in the body. Let us reconsider our ways, our thoughts and our attitudes. Remember whose we are. We are not our own. We were bought with a price. And that price was Jesus' life. The shedding of His blood was the only thing that could redeem us from the penalty of sin.

Because God is love we must reconsider our ways. Because God is love He will, through us, bring peace. If we refuse to honor the Son, (Jesus, the Christ), we are refusing to honor the Father who sent Him. Reconsider our thoughts. Reconsider how we handle and work with others.

Seek to be included in His greater glory. Seek to be a committed servant of the true and living God, our Father and Creator.

Seek to desire and reach for the greater glory of the Lord, our God.

CHAPTER 20

GOOD TIMES

"The world is changed by your example, not by your opinion."
– Paulo Coelho

During the last few chapters of writing this book, the world is experiencing a global quarantine resulting from the Coronavirus. More than six million people have been affected. There have been numerous lay offs, because businesses are not able to continue with the stringent rules needed to control the virus, millions of people have died following this outbreak; families have been made homeless due to the results of lack of employment. Our economy has suffered, the world has suffered. Only essential businesses are open, pharmacies, grocery stores, and hospitals. Restaurants are permitted to provide carryout services only. Many churches are closed. There are a few that will open and permit ten or fewer people inside at a time. Even banking has become an issue with very few banks allowing anyone in their business lobby, the outdoor drive throughs have exceptionally long lines with people trying to handle their business and personal affairs.

Many school systems have shut down for the remainder of the year. With parents having to teach their own children or at the least, help them with online studies, I am hearing people voice their complaints about not knowing the subject area themselves, with some even not having a computer in their home, let alone helping their children.

People are walking around looking as if they are trying out for an apocalyptic science fiction movie. Wearing face masks and gloves. I even saw a woman using a pull up on her head as a face mask. Now, do not get the impression that I am mocking this process. I am not. I am merely making a point. Prior to this pandemic, we took our freedoms for granted. When we could go to church to worship we did not. When we could go to the movies with our families, we did not. When we could spend quality time working with our children, we did not. When we could go for a leisurely drive through the countryside, we did not. When we could go to the grocery store to purchase specific items for someone who may have been older or less fortunate, we did not.

All of these freedoms we took for granted. All of these 'good times' we wasted. We became selfish and egotistical. Thinking only of ourselves and the 'more' we wanted. This pandemic, this disease, this unfortunate situation has caused us to come together as a people, as a nation, as a family. I trust more of us are beginning to think about the luxuries that we have. The freedoms that we used to enjoin and the challenge that we now experience. We took the 'good times' for granted.

Folks are talking more about God now then before the pandemic. But is that their heart or their fear. Maybe its just because they are tired of the circumstances. Just because they are being inconvenienced. All the time things were going well in our lives did we give God a second thought. Did we, at least, talk about His power; His goodness; His grace? Did we give any real consideration to what the death of Jesus meant to our salvation? Or, now, our lives and living?

Or were we just focusing on what we thought was our salvation? Our jobs. Our education. Our personal knowledge, skills and abilities. All the times we believed our jobs were secure. All the times we felt we were in charge. What we called, the 'good times'.

One day, when Jesus was on his way to Jerusalem, he passed through the midst of Samaria and Galilee where he met a group of ten men who were lepers. These men looked up at Jesus and asked Him to have mercy on them. Jesus instructed them to go show themselves to the priest. The scripture says, 'as they went, they were cleansed'. (St. Luke 17:11-19). Yet, only one came back to give Jesus thanks.

Will you be the one that will return to thank the Lord for saving your life, saving your family, saving your friends and others from this deadly virus? Will you be the one that will just say, Lord, I thank you for helping me recognize the 'good times' in all of this? Or will you be like the nine that were healed and just left?

So, where do we go from here? Are we focused on living a life that pleases the Lord? Do we live each day with eternity in mind or are we just so busy enjoying everything we have going on around us that we walked away from our focus on eternity? It is so easy to get caught up in the 'good times' that we lose your spiritual sensibilities. We lose sight on our purpose for life. One of the greatest challenges of our life is not to trust God when things are going downhill but to hold on to Him when they are gusting upward. Trust in God is required for success in both directions.

There will always be people who will not understand how much it costs to endure and survive bad times. This includes relatives and other loved ones. They do not always understand how tenacious you have to be to endure suffering and affliction. They do not understand how tough you have to be in your spirit and in your soul and how much it takes out of you to survive diseases, and afflictions, and turmoil, and chaos. But what they do not understand is that even when you are expecting something good to happen, it costs you something.

I heard someone define hope as 'the good thing that makes you be able to stand all the bad things'. Hope costs you something. Expectation costs you something. It takes something for you to stand in a position of readiness, expecting good things to happen, that don't. The Bible says that '*hope deferred maketh the heart sick*". Prov. 13:12 KJV Anytime hope is delayed, it will make you sick. Let me explain this thing. I thought that by now, I would have been married. I had planned a wedding for my twenties and now I am in 42, the numbers have reversed. And I am still by myself. Hope deferred maketh the heart sick. I thought I would have my degree but everytime I get ready to go back after my degree something sets me back. When you keep wanting something that keeps evading you, if you are not careful, it will wear you down.

To wait for something... anticipating and it never happens costs you more than somebody who wants nothing. That's why we have so many people who fall into the abyss of wanting absolutely nothing because sometimes it is easier not to want anything than it is to want it and not get it.

Some people say, well, this is the way it is. I'm just going to live like this. I am just going to lay between the rags and the dirty floors and just make the best of my situation. I'm going to prison because my father went to prison, my grandfather went to prison, his father went to prison. Some people find it easier to just give up and wait for death. They let things happen the way they happen. They are perpetually and inevitably victims of circumstances. That is not what the Lord has for us. He reminds us through the Prophet Jeremiah, *"For I know the thoughts that I think toward you, saith the Lord, thoughts of peace, and not of evil, to give you an expected end."* Jer. 29:11 (KJV)

Jesus told Peter, in St. Matthew chapter 16, verse 19, *"And I will give you the keys of the kingdom of heaven: and whatsoever thou shalt bind on earth shall be bound in heaven: and whatsoever thou shalt loose on earth shall be loosed in heaven."* In other words, that which is forbid on earth must be that which is already forbidden in heaven, and that which permit on earth must be that which is already permitted in heaven. It is Heaven that provides the loosing, not apostles, not pastors, not teachers. God in Heaven. It is the apostles and prophets who announce these things but they do not have the power to loose them. Apostles (including pastors, prophets, pastors) do have the power to bind when given that power by God, see Acts, chapter 15 verse 20. You do not have to be a victim of circumstances. You can have control over your life. How, you say? By putting your trust in God. Putting your trust in Jesus, the Christ and walking in His word. Remember, by our words we are healed. By our words we are condemned.

This is not to say that there will not be challenges. There will always be challenges from time to time. There will be some disappointments in all of our lives. There will be some difficult times. But these challenges, these disappointments do not have to be get the better of us. They do not have to take precedence over our souls. It is to remind you that with God, all things are possible. It is to remind us that God can keep us. That He will keep, whose mind is stayed on Him.

The authority to open the doors of the Christian world was given to Peter who used that authority for Jews on the day of Pentecost. He also used this authority for Gentiles in the house of Cornelius in the book of Acts. The keys that Jesus spoke about are symbols of authority and ruling power. God gives us a responsible position with the power to make decisions. When we accept Christ as our Saviour, we become heirs and joint-heirs with Christ. We have the opportunity to be guided by the Keeper, the Holy Spirit. To be taught and understand the Word of the Lord. He gives us wisdom. He gives us understanding for the interpretation of His Word.

Whatever we bind on earth shall be bound in heaven. Whatever we loose on earth shall be loosed in heaven. Let us bind the hand of the enemy in the name of Jesus. Let us loose the hand of the Lord in the lives of our fellow believers, in the lives of those who would otherwise be lost. In the lives of those who are seeking more of Him.

Heaven responds to us. Heaven binds what we bind and loses what we lose. If enough of us come together to bind the hand of the enemy, whether the enemy is an illness, a job, a lack of food; a father; a mother; a friend. It does not matter what the situation is. When we reconsider our ways toward God, we win!

Let us enjoy the good that is Christ. The good times of a life in peace and joy. Learn to enjoy a life that is the Kingdom of God. A life with hope and despair. Let us learn that in Christ, we move and live and have our being. The Good Life!

CHAPTER 21

SEASON FAITH

"To everything there is a season, and a time to every purpose under the heaven:"

– Eccl. 3:1 KJV

King Solomon was the wisest man on the earth. He was given wisdom and understanding by God. In his exercise of this wisdom, he provided life's order of events as written in the third chapter of the Book of Ecclesiastes. Here, Solomon reflects on what he believes is God's design for His creations and reasons that all of life's events are divinely appointed. Everyone experiences at a season of faith during their lifetime. In fact, more than one.

Has there ever been a time in your life when you needed, I mean really needed a miracle. Can you remember a time when no one could provide what you needed but God. There are times in all of our lives when situations; experiences, trauma; you know, the vicissitudes of life will happen that you will only be able to get through it because of God. Have you ever felt like you were between a rock and a hard place? Well, may I let you in on a little secret. I have been there, several times. And so will you if you are blessed to live long enough. This is not to sound like I am wearing a badge of honor. Not at all. However, it is to boast in the mighty handiwork of God.

I had been married five years. My husband was in a printer apprenticeship training program so his salary was minimal. My daughter was not yet a year old. I was working with the Federal government in a clerical capacity. I earned less than $24,000 a year. But it was more than I had ever earned in my life. We had just purchased a small two-bedroom house in the District of Columbia. We believed we were now on our way to coming out from under a heritage of less than. We were homeowners. We lived in upper Northwest. Which then, was the place to be. We were no longer apartment dwellers. We had struggled and saved to get to this point. In our minds, we thought we were on our way to our dream goal. We were moving up. Not yet, George Jefferson's moving up!

Then, one day while on my way home from work, as I usually would, I stopped at my grandmother's. I would always check on her on my way home. My daughter had not yet been picked up. My husband would normally pick her up since he got off earlier. I called my husband (no cell phones then) to find out where he was and if he was alright. He did not answer.

I cannot say that I was exercising the prophetic ability at that time. I did not even know the Spirit of Prophecy really existed save in the scriptures. I took it to be the flight or fight instinct that we are born with and that takes over with something is going wrong that we cannot explain but I now know was the Spirit of the Lord. The Spirit of the Lord impressed upon me to leave my child with my grandmother and take a cab home, not the bus which is what I normally would do. The Lord cleared the highway. If you live in the District of Columbia or any metropolitan city, you know what rush hour traffic can be like. But God held back the traffic.

The closer I got to our house, a strong sense of urgency came over me. Even as I unlocked the door, my heart felt like it was ripping from my body. I found my husband on the floor. He was breathing but his breathing was shallow. I ran to the phone and called the ambulance.

My husband was rushed to the hospital with sirens blasting. What happened? My mind was racing. Had he been sick and failed to tell me? So many thoughts were going on in my head as we were weaving in and out of traffic.

After undergoing many tests, it was determined that he had suffered a stroke. He was only twenty-six. How could this be. He was hospitalized for nine months. He had to learn how to walk and talk again. He had to learn how to wash his face, brush his teeth. Hold a spoon. Remember to swallow. During this time, we did not have the benefit of his salary since he had not yet started earning a salary but a stipend for school. Since he was not in school, there was only what I could earn. To make ends meet, (or at least to try) I worked all day at the Department of Justice and then ironed other people's clothes. It was a struggle. I was always concerned about the welfare of my child and my husband. If I lost the house, what and where would we go? How could I tell my grandmother the struggle that I was having. She, herself, was in her sixties at that time. (That's when I thought sixty was old.)

I refused to say anything to my husband since he was already sick. When he was able to speak some, he would ask me how things were going. Was I okay? Of course, my answer was, always, 'we are fine. Just rest and get better. You need your strength so you can get therapy and come home'. I did not want him to worry about us.

In my head, my mind kept saying **GOD HAS US!!** Admittedly, however, my heart was not feeling so very good about this situation. However, I had was a promise that He (God) would intervene.

I had to believe what I was hearing coming from within. I was tired of juggling. I was tired all the time. I would go to see my husband at the hospital before I went to work. I was TIRED!! I had to keep up a strong front, a straight face. I did not want him to know how tired I was. Or how desperate we were. Nor that I had to take in someone's laundry to keep paying bills. To keep food on the table, to purchase baby food and diapers. There were many nights, I would cry myself to sleep, just because I was so tired of trying to keep all the balls in the air. My daughter needed a full-time mother. Not an always tired one.

I received a letter from the mortgage company letting me know that I had thirty days to pay the arrears of the mortgage or we would be evicted. I could not let my husband know this. I was afraid he would suffer another stroke or worse, experience a heart attack and die. I did not know who to turn to for help. Certainly, not my grandmother. My mother had nothing. My sisters and brothers were of no assistance. His family was of no assistance. Yes, these same people who were in my house staying almost every weekend after we were married. My brother-in-law who would boast about his business enterprise and how much he was making. No one offered a hand or a penny. My husband was a proud man. He would not want me to 'ask' anyone for help especially his family. But I had no choice.

The church to which he had given so much of his time and money did not even send him a card. Or a balloon. The pastor and church membership knew my husband had suffered a stroke. They knew I had no other means of keeping things going. I told the pastor I was taking in laundry to help me pay my bills. I asked if he would discuss it with his wife to let me do their laundry. I never received an answer. I was willing to do whatever was necessary to keep a roof over my daughter's head and have a place to bring my husband when he did get discharged. There was no help. No one offered any assistance. No one delivered a basket, a box, or offered a meal. I was alone. Or so I thought.

That night, I talked with the Lord. I prayed. I was reminded that Job had suffered greatly; that Job had lost everything he had, children, cattle, property, his wife and even suffered affliction in his body. But he never lost his faith in God. I was reminded about the story of King Hezekiah who was sick unto death. And the prophet Isaiah came to him, and said, *"Thus saith the Lord, Set thine house in order: for thou shalt die, and not live."* 2 Kings 20:1 KJV.

The scripture went on to say that King Hezekiah turned his face to the wall and prayed to the Lord, reminding the Lord how he had walked with him in truth and with a perfect heart, and had done that which was good in His sight. Before the prophet could get out of the courtyard, the scripture lets us know that the Lord spoke to the prophet, again. Isaiah was told by God to return to King Hezekiah that He, the Lord, had heard his prayer and had seen his tears. That He, the Lord would heal him on the third day and that he (King Hezekiah) should go to the house of the Lord. He was also told that he would add fifteen (15) years to his life and that he, the Lord would bring the city out of the hand of the king of Assyria.

With that reminder, I proceeded. I had to 'gird up my faith'. I went to church, as always. I gave my tithes and offerings as always. Yes, as tight as things were, I still believed in tithing and giving. I believed that the Lord would bless us and get us out of this situation so long as I kept my faith in Jesus as my Savior. So long as I continued to show His love toward people even during my own setbacks. I took this page from King Hezekiah's life. I believed I was living a holy life. I was committed to the work and Word of the Lord. I was not committing any of the common everyday sins that we usually mention. I am sure there were some weights, if not sins, that I may have taken by omission but certainly not by deliberate commission. I repented no matter which. I rededicated my life to Christ that day. That moment. That night, I slept well.

The day before I was scheduled to be evicted, I ran into a former classmate. He had always been a good friend during college. He said, Cuffie, you don't look well. What's wrong. I began to cry. I had not told anyone outside of the church and family. I was trying to be loyal to my husband's wishes. But at this moment, I could not hold back. I explained the situation. He said, I will give you the money you need. I said, I will only accept the money if it is a loan, with no strings attached. He said, no strings. He gave me the money. The next day, when the city came to put the notice on the door and lock us out, I was able to give them the full back payment. God is good!! He hears our earnest prayers. He answers. He healed our financial situation.

This was truly a miracle. Nothing else changed in my life. My salary did not change. My husband was still hospitalized. He had no salary coming in. I was still taking in laundry. But I was never late, again on my mortgage. My child never went without food. I never went to bed hungry. My husband, after a while, began to get his mind back. Truly the Lord worked a miracle out of what some believe to have been a "plague".

This was my season of trust. My season to persevere. My season to believe. My season of faith. The scripture says, "*the just shall live by faith*" Hab. 2:4(b) KJV. Paul reiterates that same word, when he spoke to the saints in Rome, (Romans 1, verse 17- KJV). While I did not claim to be 'just' because I did not have a full understanding of what 'just' meant then, but I was assured that I was saved by the grace of God through faith in Christ. I imagined I could hear Jesus' soft but assuring voice, saying, "have faith and doubt not'. St. Matt. 21:21 (KJV)

Love works. Tithing works. Giving works. Prayer works. The Lord is a keeper. He is the shade upon our right hand. He surrounds His like the mountains surround Jerusalem. Not only did the Lord provide for the mortgage, he touched my husband's brain and refreshed his speech after about six weeks. He still was not able to form all of his words but we could piece together what he was trying to say. He still could not walk, but in another three months, he could hold a spoon. He was more alive than before. We had Jesus. We had hope. More importantly, Jesus had us!

God truly showed Himself powerful. I have to maintain my faith in God. I went about encouraging everyone I met that God is a deliverer. He is the same today as He was yesterday. His Word, His promise is true. He is a keeper! He is a deliverer. He is a healer. He is a Savior.

King Solomon said "[T]o everything there is a season and a time to every purpose under the heaven." I had just learned what that passage meant. All things have a season, a time to be in effect. But it is God who provides the message for that season. We are urged to hear the message. Urged to listen carefully to understand, the meaning for the season. But let me give you a hint, here. Even if you do not know the meaning for the season, hang in there. It will be evident when you are ready to receive it.

Whatever the enemy meant for evil against you, God will turn it around for your good. God will touch the neighbor. He will touch the heart of the supervisor. He will soften the heart of the bill collector. He will make a way out of no way. Why, because He is GOD!!. It is not because we have done something so great. It is not because we have been so good. But because His mercies are new every morning.

We listen to ABC, NBC, CBS, CNN, Facebook, Twitter and our co-workers, but we need to listen to God. If we are not willing to listen to Him in quiet times, we certainly will struggle to hear His voice when there is upheaval going on. We need to get in the practice of hearing His voice. Do not wait until your back is up against a wall. Learn to hear Him now, while it is yet day, for when night comes, we will panic and will not be able to hear.

We have a tendency to sit back and watch the 'happenings' passing judgment without realizing we are doing exactly what the enemy wants us to do. Get a song in your heart during hard times. "Down through the years, the Lord's been good to me." Oh, yes! When I remember how far He has brought me. When I remember that it was Him who brought me over, brought me out, brought me through. Thresholds to greater glory require passing the test.

Seasons have a time limit. Every event has a life span. We do not know the exact length but we do know that He knows. And as long as we stay in Him the length of the season does not matter. I had to learn that Jesus is my source of joy. Yes, I loved my husband but I had to love Jesus more. It was Jesus who kept me through this period, this season. And I knew it would be Jesus who would take me through the next one. In fact, it was learning about the love of Christ that enabled me to learn how to love my husband.

Inner peace begins the moment when you choose
Not to allow another person or event to control
your emotions.

Once I understood the key to the puzzle. The key to being happy. The key to success. I could move forward. What is the key? Jesus. Jesus rewards the faithful. He brings hope to the downtrodden. He brings joy where there is sadness. I appreciate the seasons in my life. I could not always say that. I had to learn to appreciate the seasons. Seasons give us a period of growth and rest. Just like plants. Without seasons there is no growth of the seed. Even in the winter, the seed is alive under the earth. There will be winter seasons in your life. Learn to rest in the winter.

Learn to work with the season so that you will be able to enjoy the fruit in due time. We do not appreciate watermelon in the winter. They are not as sweet. But, my God, do we eat plenty of them in the summer! Why, because watermelon is a summer fruit. It is sweetest in its rightful season.

It is easy to become discouraged when everything seems to be going wrong at the same time. It is easy to lose track of faith when it appears that everything is against you. Sometimes you will need to ask God to give you a glimpse of your summer fruit to encourage you to stay focused.

You may not have the faith of the Hebrew boys who were placed in the fiery furnace, but you are encouraged that even if He chooses not to do something, it does not mean He cannot do it. Develop season faith. Faith that works through seasons, because of seasons, and in spite of seasons.

During one of Apostle Paul's trips in Ephesus, he found a group of twelve followers of Jesus. The first thing he asked them was "Did you receive the Holy Spirit since you believed?" Acts 19:2 KJV . They responded, no. In fact, they had not even heard of any 'Holy Spirit'. What was going on. Was this just a season they had gone through. Were the supposed to have received this 'Holy Spirit' after being baptized? What should or could they have expected?

Paul asked them under what name they were baptized. They said, of John (the Baptist). Was there a difference? We are told that it is important to be baptized but do we understand the reason why. While, baptism in the water does not save us from our sins, Paul informed them that John's baptism was to help them understand they were born in sin and shaped in iniquity. John offered repentance from sin. He taught them that they were to turn to Jesus the Anointed One. Understanding that we are baptized in water to represent the newness of our lives after turning away from our sinful state. It is the outward admission to the world that we accept Christ, the Anointed One, as our personal Savior.

This reckoning began a new season in the lives of these twelve individuals. After their encounter with Paul and his explanation of baptism, Paul offered them baptism in the name of Jesus, the Christ. And when Paul laid hands upon them, the Holy Spirit came upon them, and they spoke with tongues, and prophesied.

This new life, this Keeper, this power was now in them. They experienced a change in their spiritual state. A change in their language towards Him, their Lord, Jesus Christ. This is what receiving Christ is all about. Receiving a new look; a new lease; a new Word; and a new World in which to live the life of love through Christ.

This season is so important in our lives. This season is imperative! To live a life of agape love. A love that surpasses all understanding. A love that forgives and forgets. A love that causes us to lose the weight of other people's opinions. Accepting Christ as our personal Savior and receiving the, the Holy Ghost.

Seasons are important. Each season has its purpose. Embrace them. Learn from them.

We cannot become vessels of honor without season faith. We cannot cross thresholds without seasoned faith.

CHAPTER 22

BLESS ME INDEED

Oh, that you would bless me indeed, and enlarge my territory, ...
– 1 Chron. 4:10 KJV

It is important to focus on Jesus, the Christ. It is important to know that it is because Jesus gave His life for us that we have an opportunity to live. That our sins are covered. That our discretions have been washed away. Focus on Him. Make Jesus number one in our lives.

The story of Jabez is very short. He was not a warrior. He was not a king. He was not even a shepherd. His name meant overcame with sorrow. However, scripture lets us know that Jabez was more honorable than his brethren. Jabez' short story is found in the Book of 1st Chronicles and is presumed to be written by the Prophet Ezra. Nonetheless, he prayed to God. His life and prayer only covered two verses in the Old Testament. The book, "The Prayer of Jabez" written by Mr. Bruce Wilkinson was a best seller. It was a small book of less than ninety pages but it had a monumental effect on the lives of people all over the world. In our church, we taught from that little book for six weeks but the impact still remains today. I thank God for Mr. Wilkinson and the wisdom he was given to share with us this powerful short story and words of inspiration. I thank God for putting the revelation into his head and hand. I thank God for the publishers that decided to publish it and pray that they continue to be blessed to accept other new writers to bring a word of wisdom and hope to believers and those who just need a little help to understand and push forward. Whenever lives can be changed for the better, it is a testament to God's glory.

If we are to become vessels of honor, we need to take another look at this little prayer with the desire that it would continue to have life-changing impact, again. We can never get enough of the eye-opening, life changing power of Christ in our lives.

How can we ask the Lord to bless us if we are not willing to bless Him. Blessing Him must be first. We were created to give God praise. To honor Him with the fruit of our lips. Honor Him with our daily living. Honor Him with the fruit of our hands. David said, "Let everything that has breath, praise ye the Lord." Ps. 150:6. KJV The Passion Translation terms it this way, "Let everyone everywhere join in the crescendo of ecstatic praise to Yahweh! Hallelujah! Praise the Lord!" Everyone, everywhere. That means all people. When the King James Version says, 'everything' I believe that includes, trees, flowers, birds, bees, animals of all kinds, foliage everywhere, the sun, the moon, the stars, all things.

There can be no closeness, there can be no harmony without man giving honor to his Creator. The desire to love God, the desire to worship God is worth nothing without action. As a twelve year old, I found learning about Christ interesting. I felt that I was finally receiving what I had been missing for so long.

Yes, I attended church prior to this but there was something gravely different. I knew something was missing. But I did not know what it was. My grandmother's pastor would give the sermon but this was different. Listening to this young minister, this young pastor, there was a life in His words that changed something inside me. There was an enlightenment that caused a settling in my heart. There was a fire that had been started inside of me. All along, I knew there was more than what I was hearing and receiving. The scripture says, seek and ye shall find. I thank the Lord, that I kept seeking. I found Him. It was my season.

The Bible is replete with examples of great faith. Abraham, who became the father of many nations; David, a shepherd boy, who was anointed king three times before becoming king of Israel; Elijah and Elisha who were both great prophets, healing, raising the dead, and calling down fire from heaven; Job, who endured the loss of his entire family, his property, his cattle and was gravely afflicted in his body but never once did he blame or mock God; Stephen who was stoned for being a Christian; Paul whose original name was Saul, whom was struck blind by the Lord and began to work for the same Lord he persecuted others for following. I wanted this faith. I wanted faith that would be sufficient to heal the sick, no matter what the illness. I sought faith that would bring prosperity to those who were suffering from financial lack. I sought faith that would persuade others to accept Christ as their personal Savior. I sought *that* faith that was once delivered unto the saints. However, in all of my seeking, I never considered the cost.

Without rain nothing grows,
Learn to embrace the storms of life.

Before any goal can be reached, before the next level, there is always a test. Sometimes I thought that I would never get to the next level. It seemed like there was always a test. I believe that we sometimes experience our tests and trials before we even recognize our goal. Before we even know our purpose.

I left my family at the age of fifteen. I got tired of the alcoholism, the fights, the cursing, the gambling and so much other stuff. I became so nervous that I required medication. I could not think anymore. I wanted out. Where, O'Lord, I would pray. Where?

I was not the prettiest girl on the block. Far from it. I was skinny, plain, with very thin curly hair, that I did not appreciate at the time. That's another story. It was not enough that I had gifts that I could not understand. My life was complicated by being a nerd or bookworm as my fellow peers would call me. I wanted to fit in and be accepted. That did not happen. They played bad games at my expense. I ended up being a loner. Not trusting people.

It wasn't until I entered high school that I finally found two girls, Dolores and Gwendolyn, who accepted me for me. That is when I learned the value of friendship. These two young ladies encouraged me to be me. I was a good student. I was quiet. The Lord had blessed me with a great imagination. I wrote and directed our senior graduating class play. I was elected to be Principal for the Day in my final year of high school. I even ran for student office. This was something I would normally not have done, at all, prior to meeting these friends.

When Dolores learned that she had cancer and would require an amputation of her arm, in twelfth grade, she was devastated. She did not want to graduate with one arm. Gwendolyn and I received permission from the principal to go around the school and collect money to help purchase a prosthetic for her so she would not feel badly about graduating without an arm. I believed it was then that I had found my calling, my purpose. I believed I was called to help others.

I want you to understand that requesting expanded territory will cost you. I did not know how or in what area I would help. But this one thing I did know, I would help. During my teenage years, we were taught that we could only be teachers, nurses and typists. I was placed in the business track in my high school. I wanted to learn how to cook and sew like my grandmother who never completed high school but she was the smartest lady I knew. God had other plans.

So, I followed what was set before me. I learned shorthand and typing, receiving many class awards. My English classroom grades were so high I was excused from the final exam. I could not understand why I was studying business when I wanted to learn how to cook and sew to help out at home. Nevertheless, I continued as I was taught to be obedient and follow the rules.

I tried nursing but unfortunately, or rather, fortunately for the potential patients, I learned early that that wonderful and exciting profession was not for me. I have an intense fear of needles. Thinking about getting one causes my blood pressure to rise. One day, I saw Congressional Representative Shirley Chisholm, the first Black woman elected to the United States Congress in 1968, on television. She represented New York's 12th congressional district for seven terms from 1969 to 1983. She was a politician, an educator and author. I decided that if she could do this, if she was willing to make sacrifices to show that Black women could be more than teachers and typists, the least I could do was follow her example, as closely as I could. So I set out to do just that. I studied Ms. Chisholm's history. She was a woman of purpose. She was dedicated to what she set her mind to.

It was an uphill battle. My grandmother did not understand why I wanted to go to college. She did not understand why I wanted to go to law school. She thought high school was sufficient. I tried to explain to her that we, as a people, needed more now than when she grew up. We will need education to compete for better jobs and to help others know that there is hope. That no one has to remain poor and destitute. Waiting for handouts and hand-me-downs.

People were trying to discourage me from going to college. Even in the church. I was told that it is not for me. That all you need is Christ and the church. Yet, the leaders encouraged and paid for their children's higher educational endeavors. I did not have parents that could help me or assist me as to what I needed to look for in a college or a particular career path. They did not have such luxury themselves. God had given me a new family. When I started working for the Federal government, my first position was as a clerk in a government warehouse at the Navy Yard working for the General Services Administration. The family (leadership employees) were Jewish by birth and belief. They taught me. God allowed them to teach me their culture for a reason. I believe He wanted me to learn about Him. To learn who He is at each level of His being. El Elyon ("Most High"). The El-Shaddai ("Almighty God"). The Elohim ("The Strong One"). Yahweh ("I Am"). Pater ("Father"). There are so many more attributes and characters of God. These are merely a few to help you seek out whom He is to you.

I did not let that stop me. I had a goal and I was going to push forward. I knew the Lord would work things out. I graduated high school in 1963. In 1964, I entered the government service where the Lord placed me in an office with Jewish backgrounded people. They took me under their wing. They helped me prepare a roadmap for reaching my goal. They even gave me information for seeking out colleges that would accept minority students. That was the first time I had heard about scholarships.

Just when I was ready to move forward with the paperwork after completing volunteer public service to be added to my application, Dr. Martin Luther King was assassinated. This event took my efforts and, I am sure, a couple hundred other potential students, backward for a period of time. But I had to stay focused. It was imperative that I stay faithful and focused on what the Lord had shown me. I knew there would be some difficulties. I knew there would be some hardships. This was difficult. This was not just ignoring the naysayers in my life. This was not just about letting those who were against me to win. It was about proving to myself that I trusted the Word of God for my future. That I did not have to live the way my grandmother, my mother, or aunts and other family members had lived. It was not about continuing the circle of poverty and a life that meant nothing. It was about making a difference. Knowing that the Lord had given me what I needed to make a change in my family's history and their future.

I asked that the Lord bless me and enlarge my territory. I remembered that it was necessary to count the cost. I had to be sure that I was willing to do the work and walk the walk that is necessary to be ready to serve. My desire to 'be' the blessing that the Lord told me I could, should and would be keeps me searching His Word. Keeps me striving to be a living example of what Christ has called each of us to be.

David wrote in Psalm one, "blessed is the man that walketh not in the counsel of the ungodly nor standeth in the way of sinners, nor sitteth in the seat of the scornful." (KJV) I wanted to be that 'man' that person whom God would bless. I resolved that I would not walk in the counsel of ungodly people. I would not become a stumbling block for a sinner to refuse to accept Christ as his or her personal Savior. I would not sit in judgment of others, nor be scornful against others who may have better. I wanted to be 'that blessed man'.

I reasoned how can I ask God to broaden my territory if I could not handle and be fruitful where I was. I had to prove myself to myself. I had to prove to the Lord that I was worthy. God promotes those He can trust. Can I be trusted with His Word? Can I be trusted with His power? In order to be a blessing, I had to walk worthy of the vocation to which God was and is calling me to.

I am encouraged to know that if God is for me no thing or no one can have control over me or my life or what is mine. Why, because God has dispatched His angels to take charge over me. When we seek to enjoy a closer relationship with Him. When we seek to live everyday according to His word, He allows us a better glimpse into His realm of revelation. A better look into our present and our future with Him. Putting God first is primary. Nothing comes before giving Him glory.

I encourage you to seek first the kingdom of God and His righteousness. Putting Christ first in your life. All other things will be added unto you. Be the living example; the living epistle; the blessing that others can benefit from. Be all that you can be in Him. Remembering to give Him glory in all things. Be ready to be a vessel of honor.

CHAPTER 23

WHO CAN
SEPARATE ME

"What shall we say to these things? If God be for us, who can be against us?"

– Rom. 8: 31 KJV

Today is Palm Sunday. Yes, I know people are waiting to hear an Easter Week sermon. But this is what the Lord has given me. I am reminded of Theology classes. We know there are 66 books that make up the canonized Bible. There is a requirement to learn portions of two languages used in the Bible, Greek and Hebrew. There is much reading and lots of memorization.

I want to look at this passage of scripture in a slightly different way. I will use the usual 'who' references to set the stage for this particular revelatory word. As anyone knows who has attended theology school, there is a lot of material that needs to be covered in the short time of study that is offered. There are a number of interesting and enlightening books on theology. There is much wisdom and revelation that can be drawn from the pages of the Holy Bible. All of us have our favorite or favorites, as the case maybe. I am particularly fond of the Books of Genesis, Proverbs, Daniel and Revelation for what I call my revelatory reading. When it comes to learning how to live holy in this present life, I look to Paul's writings, in particular, the Book of Romans.

The Epistle to the Romans was the letter that the Apostle Paul wrote to the church in Rome. As all of the books of the Bible include words of wisdom and revelation, this particular missive is full of everyday living helps. Let's look at a quick breakdown. In Chapter one, he leads with, 'the world is in total depravity.' One verse lets us know that God even gives the unjust over to a depraved mind because of their sin. Depraved means having a seared conscience or the inability to distinguish between right and wrong. We thank God for a conscience.

In Chapter two, Paul told the church in Rome that God tried to fix this depraved world with a law that had a bunch of rules that the people could not keep. Chapter three introduces us to Abraham, the Father of many nations. In Chapter four, Paul states, if we have the faith of Abraham, we can call those things that are not as if they were.

In Chapter three, Paul re-introduces us to Abraham (Abram). By the way, his name did not change until after the promised son was born. The Father of many nations. You remember. He and his wife were, too old to have children naturally. The Lord promised him that he and his wife, Sarai would bear a child in their old age. Of course, Sarai laughed. Which she denied. And why not, Abram was in his eighties. For many years, nothing happened. Sarai was tired of waiting. She offered her husband Hagar, her handmaid. Was this because she actually believed Abraham could not produce a child so she had nothing to lose, or was it because she did not believe that God's word was going to come true without her assistance? Whatever was her true reasoning, we may not know. But the fact is, the handmaid became pregnant with Abraham's son. But it was not the promised son. The couple was rebuked and then had to wait, again.

After Hagar conceived, Sarai became jealous and reduced her to her former status as a slave and handmaiden. She was no longer Abraham's concubine. Sarai acknowledged her wrong to Abram and stated that she became upset when Hagar would flaunt her pregnancy before her. Sarai began to deal harshly with Hagar. Hagar left the village. It was after Hagar left the company of Abraham that she had an encounter with the Lord, herself. She was told to return to Sarai, her mistress, and to submit under her hands. Hagar, at the instruction of the angel of the Lord, returned with a blessing over her and her child.

Hagar gave birth to a son, whom she called Ishmael. Ishmael in Hebrew means "God hears". I want you to know that God hears your cries. He sees your tears. If we have performed as we were told, if we are living according to the Word of the Lord; treating others with love and compassion God has promised to be with us.

Life is not always easy. We can do what we know is right. We can be obedient to those who have rule over us. We can, sometimes, get a little beside ourselves because of a blessing that is not due us but has been provided for us. Yet, God gives us the opportunity to return. Who shall separate you from the love of God?

Ishmael always comes before Isaac.

We get caught up on the 'who' of adversity. The 'who' of difference of opinion. The 'who' that is a person to tear us down. Or challenge our faith. Shall we continue for a few minutes?

Thirteen years passed after the birth of Ishmael before Sarai became pregnant. Giving birth to Isaac, the promised son. Abram was one hundred years old when Isaac was born. We are reminded that what may look like the blessing does not have to be the blessing that the Lord promised. Ishmael always comes before Isaac. Ishmael does not have to be a bad thing, person or action, just not the promised thing, person or action.

Remember to seek God at every turn. Ask yourself, does it match the Word of the Lord. Is this the real blessing that I am to receive or is it a tease of what is to come. Be ready to hear the voice of the Lord. Who shall separate you?

In Chapter four, we are reminded that if we have the faith Abraham possessed we can call those things that were not as though they are. What a statement. What a future. What a mighty work by the living

Lord. A faith that will allow those who have the strength of courage to walk out and walk in. Just think about the power this engenders. Wow! Such an understatement of life.

In Chapter five, we are told that it is by grace that we are saved through faith. Not by works. Not by looks. Not by money. Not by intelligence. Not by power. But by grace. The grace of God through faith we are saved. We have an assurance that we can live with Him in heaven.

Thinking about this begs the question, "with this knowledge and power, who shall separate us from His love"?

In Chapter six, even though we may mess up sometimes, where sin does abound, grace abounds all the more. In other words, there is more grace than mistakes. Chapter seven talks about the struggle between the flesh and the spirit. Paul said, when I would do good, evil is always present.

This brings us to Chapter 8, 'there is now no condemnation to those who are in Christ, Jesus. If God be for us, who can be against us? By the time I got to this verse, I was so excited. I could hardly sit still to write. Admittedly, I had to stop and give God a shabach praise. I could not contain myself. It is important to understand the who.

Stop worrying about the what. Get to know the Who. Jesus, the Christ is the Who on whom we should become addicted. Our relationship must be with the Who. Who can separate us. No one. No man. No woman. No thing.

Stop looking at the 'who' that is really the what. It is always the what that will come to separate us. We become so easily derailed by our fleshly desires.

You will find out the Bible is always about a who. It is not about a what. Look at Genesis, the book of beginnings. It identifies and emphasizes the who. The who is God. The Creator. The Alpha and the Omega. He is the Beginning and the End.

If you are not addicted to Him you are addicted to them. When the wrong people lead your life, wrong things start happening. When the right people enter your life, right things start happening.

Unbelief sets you up for failure before you even start.

When the enemy recognizes that he cannot stop us from serving the true and living God. He starts throwing 'things' into our path. These 'things' become the 'whats and the thems'. Whats such as, pain, sickness, setbacks, viruses, cancer, diabetes, heart disease and I am sure he thinks of many other 'thems'. Stop getting excited about the 'thems'. It is not the 'thems' that should have control over you.

God foreknew us. He knew our ending before our beginning. He knew what our middle was going to look like before we were even born. Romans, chapter 8 verse 30, *"Moreover whom he did predestinate, them he also called: and whom he called, them he also justified: and whom he justified, them he also glorified."* God only calls the things he wants. He called you and me. He chose us from the beginning of eternity.

The prefix 'pre' means before and 'destine' means in. So the verse would read, He called us before we were in our mother's womb. It was already decided that we would be chosen to serve in the Lord's army while we were not even a twinkle in the thoughts of our parents. God knew whom He wanted. He knew whom He would call.

God searches our hearts not just to uncover what is wrong, but to fulfill the true desire of our hearts to be fully His. Grace triumphs over judgment. God seals us with His mark. (See Col. 4:4; and Heb. 2:11) The Apostle Paul reminds us, as he reminded the saints in his epistle to the Hebrews, "…let us lay aside every weight, and the sin which doth so easily beset us, and let us run with patience, the race that is set before us." Heb. 12:1(b) KJV We are urged to live as one who has died to every form of sin and impurity. We are encouraged to live as one who died to diseases and desires for forbidden things, including the desire for wealth, which is the essence of idol worship, if that desire will take us from the peaceful presence of God. When you live in these vices you ignite the anger of God against these acts of disobedience.

What can we say to these things? Shall tribulation, or distress, or persecution, or famine, or nakedness, or peril, or sword separate us from the love of God? Paul says, so emphatically, Nay. In all these things we are more than conquerors through him that loved us. Paul reiterated his commitment to God. "For I am persuaded that neither death, nor life, nor angels, nor principalities, nor powers, nor things present, nor things to come, nor height, nor depth, nor any other creature, shall be able to separate us from the love of God, which is in Christ Jesus our Lord. Rom. 8:37-39 KJV.

Our relationship must be with the Who. The capital "W". Who can separate us. No one. No man. No woman. No situation. No circumstance. Nothing can separate me from Christ. Set your mind on the "who" which is Christ. If we do that, we cannot fail. We cannot be defeated by the enemy because we have the 'Who' with us. In us.

It is by the strength of this character. The strength of this resolve to commit our lives, ourselves to the word and work of our Savior that brings us to the life that is the Kingdom of God. It is imperative that we move forward in our endeavors to seek the peace of God that transcends the word through faith.

Let us not find ourselves in the same situation as Adam and Eve found themselves after they committed the sin of disobedience. In the Book of Genesis, chapter 3, verse nine, "And the Lord God called unto Adam, and said unto him, "where art thou?" Did God lose Adam and Eve?

Did He not know where they were? This God who is the author and creator of the heavens and the earth. This God who is omniscient and omnipresent. This God that is Almighty asking this question, 'where are you?'

Of course, God knew where they were. They were hiding because they discovered they were naked. Remember, Adam and Eve were created in the imagine of God. They were created in spirit form and clothe in righteousness. They had no sin. There was no sin on the earth, or in the earth. There was no reason for them to know that they had no physical covering.

When they sinned, when they disobeyed, then sin entered the earth. The balance of life was disturbed. Their connection to God was broken. No wonder God asked that fateful question, "Adam, where are you?"

We must be ever vigilant to now lose our connection with God. We should ask ourselves periodically, 'Am I still connected to my Savior?" "Am I naked?" May I suggest our daily prayer should include the following language….

Lord, help me to be the vessel you want me to be. Help me to be a Vessel of honor for your service. So that you get the glory! Search my character, search my inner desires that I might not be a liability to you and to your mission of love. Your mission to select water walkers, soldiers, guardians on the wall. Your mission to save the lost.

As you allow us to move forward with your work for the Kingdom, help us to learn to forgive those who have trespassed against us. Help us to learn to pray for those who have despitefully used us. Help us to sow love where there is hate.

Renew us to a closer walk with you, Oh God. Renew us that we may be fit for the Kingdom of Heaven. Help us, Father that you will never have to ask, "Where are you, my child?"

Amen

May the peace that is Christ be yours as you continue your journey to becoming a vessel of honor and be able to cross thresholds into greater glory.

www.ingramcontent.com/pod-product-compliance
Lightning Source LLC
Chambersburg PA
CBHW071407120626
46546CB00002B/842